AF263982

Egyptian Mythology for Beginners

The Legends of Ancient Egypt Simplified for People Who Slept Through History Class

Free Bonus from Captivating History (Available for a Limited time)

Hi History Lovers!

Now you have a chance to join our exclusive history list so you can get your first history ebook for free as well as discounts and a potential to get more history books for free!

Simply visit the link below to join.

Or, Scan the QR code!

captivatinghistory.com/ebook

Also, make sure to follow us on Facebook, X, and YouTube by searching for Captivating History.

Table of Contents

Introduction

If you slept through history class, you're not alone. History gets taught as dates, names, and facts to memorize for a test. It's presented as something dead and distant, disconnected from anything that matters to your actual life. But history isn't boring. It's just that the way it's often taught is boring.

The truth is that ancient people were just as complex, funny, weird, dramatic, and human as anyone you know today. They told wild stories, had messy family dynamics, believed things that seem bizarre to us now, and built civilizations that lasted longer than anything we've managed. Egyptian mythology gives us a window into how an entire culture made sense of existence for three thousand years. That's not boring. That's fascinating.

This book treats these myths the way they deserve—as compelling stories that shaped one of history's greatest civilizations, not as bullet points to memorize.

The Egyptian civilization lasted three thousand years. Not three hundred. Three thousand. That's longer than the time between the fall of Rome and today. Longer than Christianity has existed. The Great Pyramid of Giza was already ancient and mysterious to Cleopatra; it was older to her than she is to us.

For all those centuries, the Egyptians told stories. Stories about gods who created the world from nothing, about murder and resurrection, about epic battles that lasted eighty years, about a sun that died every night and had to be defended from a chaos serpent in the underworld. These weren't just bedtime stories. These myths formed the foundation of

Egyptian government, art, architecture, daily life, and their entire understanding of existence.

You've seen Egyptian imagery everywhere. The pyramids. The Sphinx. Mummies wrapped in linen. Gods with animal heads standing in profile on temple walls. Maybe you played an assassin in ancient Egypt in a video game or saw Brendan Fraser battle CGI scarabs in *The Mummy*. But unless you're an Egyptologist, you probably don't know the actual stories behind those images.

Here's what makes Egyptian mythology different from the Greek or Norse myths you might know better. The Greeks gave us superhero-style gods who acted like powerful, flawed humans. Zeus threw lightning bolts and cheated on his wife. Loki played pranks. These gods were basically immortal people with superpowers.

Egyptian gods were something else entirely. They represented forces of nature and cosmic principles, but they also had distinct personalities, flaws, and emotions. Ra wasn't just a powerful guy who happened to control the sun. He *was* the sun, traveling across the sky in a boat every single day, fighting for his life every single night in the underworld. But he also aged, grew tired, and could be tricked. Osiris didn't just rule the dead. He died, was dismembered, put back together, and became the template every Egyptian hoped to follow in death. These gods embodied concepts like order and chaos, life and death, flood and drought, creation and destruction while also acting as characters in stories with jealousies, schemes, and very real emotions.

And those animal heads? They weren't random. Each animal was chosen because its natural behavior or characteristics reflected the god's role. Anubis got a jackal head because jackals scavenged in cemeteries. Thoth became an ibis because ibises probed the mud of the Nile looking for food, like Thoth probed the mysteries of wisdom and magic. Sobek was a crocodile because the Nile had crocodiles, and the Nile was life itself. The Egyptians didn't think their gods literally looked like this. The animal heads were symbolic shorthand, a way to instantly communicate what each god represented.

This book will take you through the actual myths, not the Hollywood versions. You'll learn how the world was created through an act too weird to describe in polite company. You'll follow Isis as she searches all of Egypt for her murdered husband's dismembered body parts. You'll watch Horus and Set battle for the throne through competitions involving stone boats, underwater hippo fights, and a deeply uncomfortable incident involving lettuce. You'll meet the entire divine family tree, from the sun god who aged and drooled to the dwarf god who protected babies by being grotesquely ugly.

You'll also learn what Egyptians actually believed happened after death. Spoiler: it involved your heart being weighed against a feather while a monster waited to eat you if you failed the test. No pressure.

Most importantly, you'll understand why these myths mattered. Egyptian mythology wasn't entertainment. It was the operating system for an entire civilization. The pharaoh wasn't just a king; he was literally the god Horus in human form, maintaining cosmic balance. Temple priests weren't just religious officials; they were performing daily rituals to keep the sun rising and the Nile flooding. Ordinary farmers painted protective symbols on their homes because magic was as real to them as gravity is to us.

By the time you finish this book, you'll know why the Egyptians spent decades building elaborate tombs. You'll understand the stories behind the hieroglyphs. You'll be able to identify the major gods at a glance. And you'll have a sense of how these ancient people made sense of birth, death, order, chaos, and the terrifying beauty of the natural world around them.

Let's start at the beginning. The very beginning. Before the sun, before the earth, before the gods themselves. Back when there was only water, potential, and nothing else.

Chapter 1: The Beginning of Everything

The Nu: Floating in the Infinite Cosmic Soup

Before there was anything, there was nothing. But not the kind of nothing you're picturing. The ancient Egyptians imagined something weirder than empty space or darkness. They called it Nu, an infinite ocean that existed before anything else did.

Nu wasn't ordinary water. It had no surface, no bottom, and no movement. It was just endless stillness in every direction.

The strange part? Everything that would ever exist—every god, every person, every animal, every grain of sand—was already in Nu, but only as a possibility. They were like ingredients sitting in a kitchen before anyone cooks them. The Egyptians were describing a state of pure potential, where everything existed but nothing had separated into distinct forms yet. Life and death were mixed together. Light and darkness were the same thing. Order and chaos hadn't split apart. All of it just floated in the dark water, waiting.

Nu never went away. The created world was a bubble of order floating in an infinite dark ocean, with the sun traveling through Nu each night in the underworld.

This made sense to people living along the Nile. Water meant life. When the Nile's yearly flood came, fields that had been dry and dead suddenly burst with green crops. Water transformed barren land into fertile earth. So naturally, the beginning of everything would be water. But

Nu wasn't the Nile. It was something bigger and stranger. The Nile itself would eventually come from Nu, along with everything else.

The Egyptians believed that if you traveled far enough in any direction—past the deserts, past the mountains, past the edge of the known world—you'd eventually reach Nu again. The waters of chaos surrounded everything. This is why the desert was so terrifying to them. It was the edge, the place where order started to break down, where you could see the boundary between the created world and the nothing beyond.

Nu was sometimes treated as a god, but not in an active way. Nu didn't create anything. Nu didn't make choices. It just existed. The deity Nu represented the state before states existed, the condition before conditions mattered. You couldn't pray to Nu for help because Nu had no will, no personality, and no preferences. Nu simply was.

Other gods would organize things, but Nu stayed underneath it all. If creation ever failed, everything would sink back into this undifferentiated soup.

Other cultures also started their creation stories with water, but the Egyptian version is different. It's not violent or stormy. It's perfectly calm. Creation didn't start with a battle or thunder. It started with something rising up from the still surface of the endless waters. That something was Atum, and when he showed up, everything changed from possibility into reality.

But we're getting ahead of ourselves. For now, just picture darkness, silence, stillness, and infinite water holding everything that could ever be but isn't yet. That's where the Egyptian universe starts. In the Nu.

Atum and the First Sneeze: How the World Began at Heliopolis

Out of the waters of Nu, a mound appeared. It was just a small hill of dirt, rising above the infinite ocean. This was the very first piece of solid ground to exist anywhere. The Egyptians called it the Benben, and it would become one of the most sacred symbols in their religion. Every temple in Egypt would later claim to be built on the spot where the Benben first emerged. And standing on top of it, alone in the endless dark water, was Atum.

A reconstructed apex of an Egyptian pyramid representing the Benben.[1]

In some versions of the myth, the first living creature to appear on the primeval mound was the Bennu bird, a sacred heron associated with the sun's rebirth. The Bennu perched on the mound and cried out, its call breaking the eternal silence and marking the moment when time itself began. Later, the Greeks would hear stories of the Bennu and create their own version: the phoenix that dies in flames and is reborn from its ashes.

Where did Atum come from? He created himself. This is one of those ideas that ancient Egyptians were totally fine with, but it does make modern people pause. Atum just willed himself into being. He had no parents or creator. He just thought himself into reality and emerged from Nu as the first conscious being in the universe. Some texts describe him rising from a lotus flower that bloomed on the surface of Nu. Others say he simply appeared on the mound. Either way, he existed because he decided to exist.

The name "Atum" means "the complete one" or "the all." He contained everything inside himself. He was male and female, light and dark, and every possibility squeezed into one divine being. He was totality itself before anything split into separate parts. To put it very simply, Atum was the entire universe compressed into a single god standing on a tiny island of dirt.

But Atum had a problem. He was completely alone on his mound, surrounded by infinite water. So he decided to create companions.

Now comes the weird part, even by mythology standards. Atum created the next generation of gods through self-pleasure. The ancient texts are surprisingly clear about this. Some versions say he masturbated. Others say he sneezed or spat. But the basic idea is the same: Atum produced the first divine couple from his own body fluids.

The Pyramid Texts, some of the oldest religious writings in Egypt, describe how Atum took his penis in his hand and achieved orgasm. From that act of self-love, two gods burst into existence, Shu and Tefnut, the first male-female pair of gods. Shu was air, breath, and space. Tefnut was moisture and wetness. Together, they were the basic ingredients for a livable world.

Why would the Egyptians tell the story this way? It is because they saw every bodily function as natural and necessary, not shameful. The human body was sacred. Semen, spit, blood, and milk were powerful substances that carried life. Creation through body fluids made perfect sense to the ancient Egyptians. Atum was making new life from his own essence, splitting his completeness into the first pair of separate beings.

Some versions add extra details. Atum used his hand as the female part, creating a union within himself. He sneezed out Shu and spat out Tefnut. The exact mechanics changed depending on which temple told the story, but the meaning stayed the same: the first act of creation involved Atum breaking himself into parts, turning from one into many. The names even reflected this. "Shu" sounds like the Egyptian word for "empty" or "air." "Tefnut" sounds like the word for "spit" or "moisture."

Shu and Tefnut were still on the mound with their father, surrounded by the dark water. But now Atum wasn't alone. The universe had gone from one to three. And those three would soon become many more.

Atum created Shu and Tefnut, but then he lost them. They wandered off into the darkness of Nu, and Atum couldn't find them in the endless water. So, he removed his eye—yes, his actual eye—and sent it out to search for his children.

Why his eye? Well, the eye could see, search, and find what was lost. The eye had power and independence. It could act on Atum's behalf while he waited on the mound. This was the Eye of Ra, and it would become one of the most important symbols in Egyptian mythology.

The eye found them and brought them back. Atum was so happy that he wept, and from his tears, humans were created. That's the Egyptian explanation for where people came from. We're made from divine tears of joy. The Egyptians loved this story partly because of its clever wordplay. Their word for "tears" (*remut*) sounded nearly identical to their word for "people" (*remet*). We weren't the main event of creation. We were born from the gods' emotions.

But while Atum's eye was out searching, Atum created a second eye to replace it. When the original eye returned and found itself replaced, it was furious.

To calm the angry eye down, Atum put it on his forehead, where it became the uraeus, the cobra that Egyptian pharaohs would later wear as a symbol of divine protection. The eye that searched in darkness became the fiery cobra that destroys the king's enemies. Every pharaoh wore this symbol on their crown. It was a warning. "I carry the power of creation itself. Cross me and face the wrath of the first angry eye."

Atum's work wasn't finished, but he'd done the crucial first step. He'd broken unity into many parts. He'd made air and moisture, the basic ingredients for a world. And from his emotions, he'd accidentally created humanity. The age of the single, lonely god was over. Now the divine family would grow, and the created world would expand.

Shu and Tefnut would continue what Atum started, and everything would get more complex and organized. But it all began with one god, one mound, and one deeply strange creative act that brought the first beings into reality. The Egyptians never forgot this. When they built pyramids, they were recreating the Benben, the first mound rising from chaos. When they built temples, they were making sacred spaces that echoed that original island of order. The whole of civilization, in a way, was an attempt to maintain what Atum had started on that lonely hill, surrounded by dark water.

The Ennead: Meeting the "Great Nine" Family Tree

Shu and Tefnut did what gods do. They had children, and their children had children. Within a few generations, the lonely god Atum had become a family of nine deities. These nine gods were the Ennead, the great divine family of Heliopolis, and they would shape the world into something recognizable. The word "Ennead" means "group of nine."

Shu, the god of air, and Tefnut, the goddess of moisture, had the next divine pair, Geb and Nut. If Shu and Tefnut were the basic ingredients,

Geb and Nut took things further. Geb was the earth itself, solid ground rising from the water. When you stand on soil, you're standing on Geb's body. Nut was the sky, the vast space that would arch over the world and hold the stars. When you look up, you're seeing Nut's body stretched across the heavens.

Egyptian mythology does something different from most other cultures. In their version, the earth was male, and the sky was female. Compare this to almost any other mythology you know—Greek, Norse, Mesopotamian—and the earth is usually the mother while the sky or heaven is usually the father.

Why was this? We can't know for sure, but it made sense in their world. The earth was hard, solid, and firm—qualities they linked to men. The sky was vast, surrounding, and nurturing—qualities they linked to women. And Nut didn't just sit above the earth. She actively protected it. She was the mother who held the cycle of death and rebirth. Every sunset was the sun entering Nut's mouth. Every sunrise was Nut giving birth to the sun again. This happened every single day, and it would continue happening for all eternity.

Geb and Nut loved each other intensely—a little too intensely. They were locked in a permanent embrace, Nut's body arched over Geb, the two pressed together with no space between earth and sky. This created a serious problem. How could anything exist in a universe where earth and sky were crushed together? Where would the sun travel on its daily journey? Where would humans live? Where would plants grow? Everything was compressed into nothingness between the two loving deities.

Shu had to intervene. The god of air forced his way between his two children and pushed them apart. He stood with his feet planted firmly on Geb's body and his hands pressing upward against Nut's belly, creating the space between earth and sky. This space—what we call the atmosphere—was Shu himself. Every breath you take is Shu. The gap between ground and stars is Shu holding up his daughter forever, preventing the earth and sky from reaching each other.

It wasn't easy. Geb and Nut struggled against the separation. They wept and called out to each other. But Shu held firm. He had to. The created world depended on it. Some texts describe Geb's sadness at being separated from his love. His tears became the oceans. Nut's longing turned to rain, her tears falling down toward her husband below.

Artists loved showing this scene. You can see it in tomb paintings and on papyri—Geb lying on his back below, sometimes with an erect penis reaching up toward his separated wife; Nut arched above him with her hands and feet touching the edges of the earth; and Shu in the middle, arms raised, muscles straining, holding the sky goddess up. Stars dot Nut's body. Sometimes the sun god's boat is shown traveling along Nut's arched form.

Depiction of Shu separating Geb and Nut. Original artwork created around 950 BCE.[2]

But Geb and Nut's separation didn't end their relationship. They'd already conceived children during their embrace. They had five children, and they would be a central part of every myth that followed. Their names are recognizable: Osiris, Isis, Set, Nephthys, and Horus the Elder. These weren't abstract forces like their grandparents and parents. These were characters with emotions, desires, jealousies, and schemes. Egyptian mythology was shifting from cosmic creation to family drama.

We need to pause and explain something before we go too much further. There are two gods named Horus. Ancient sources sometimes treat them as the same figure and sometimes as different beings. Horus the Elder was born to Geb and Nut. He was a sky god and a god of kingship. He is not consistently included in the standard Ennead of nine gods, but in some variations, particularly regional ones, he appears as a member.

Horus the Younger was the son of Osiris and Isis, and his story dominates Egyptian mythology. He's the one who fought Set for the throne, the one whose eye became a powerful symbol, and the one every pharaoh claimed to embody. These are different gods with different roles, though Egyptians sometimes blended them together. For now, just know that Horus the Elder belongs to the fourth generation of gods, while Horus the Younger is his nephew and the one who will soon take center stage.

The birth of these five children involved some divine trickery and a gambling debt. Ra, the sun god (who was sometimes the same as Atum and sometimes treated as separate—Egyptian religion was flexible about these things), had said that Nut couldn't give birth on any day of the year. This was either punishment for her improper embrace with Geb or simply Ra being difficult and jealous. Maybe he didn't want competition from a new generation of gods.

However, this created a problem. Nut was pregnant with five children, and Ra's decree meant she couldn't give birth to them. The babies would be stuck inside her forever. Enter Thoth, the clever god of wisdom and magic. Thoth wasn't one of the Ennead—he came from a different theological tradition—but Egyptian myths often borrowed gods from other cities when they needed a specific skill set. And Thoth was famous for being clever and solving impossible problems. If anyone could find a loophole in Ra's decree, it was Thoth.

Thoth challenged the moon to a game; sources say it was senet, an Egyptian board game a bit like backgammon. Thoth was smart, and the moon was apparently a bad gambler. Thoth won, and as his prize, he took a tiny bit of light from the moon.

It doesn't sound like much, but Thoth used that stolen light to create five extra days that didn't officially belong to the calendar year. The Egyptian calendar had 12 months of 30 days each, which equals 360 days. But the actual solar year is about 365 days. Where did those extra five days come from? The ancient Egyptians say they were Thoth's gambling winnings. These five days existed outside the normal year in a kind of temporal loophole. They weren't part of the year, so Nut could give birth on them without technically breaking Ra's rule.

This myth explained why the Egyptian calendar had 365 days instead of 360. It also explained why the moon waxes and wanes since Thoth had taken some of its light. Those extra five days at the end of the year were special, sacred days when the barrier between divine and human worlds thinned. People didn't work. They celebrated. They waited to see what the year ahead would bring. And each day matched one of Nut's children being born: Osiris on the first day, Horus the Elder on the second, Set on the third, Isis on the fourth, and Nephthys on the fifth.

The birth order mattered immensely. Osiris, as the firstborn, would become king of the gods and the first pharaoh of Egypt. Set, born third, would always resent being younger than his brother. Why should Osiris rule just because he came out first? Set was stronger and more powerful. This resentment would fuel the central conflict of Egyptian mythology. Isis, born fourth, would become the greatest magician and the devoted wife of her brother Osiris. Nephthys, born last, would marry Set but sympathize with her sister.

With the birth of these five, the Ennead was complete. There were nine or ten gods, depending on which version you follow. Some sources include Horus the Elder in the count, while others do not. Egyptian religion was flexible about these details. Atum was at the top, then Shu and Tefnut, then Geb and Nut, and then Osiris, Isis, Set, and Nephthys, with Horus the Elder sometimes counted as the ninth member.

Together, they changed the universe from Atum's lonely mound into an organized world, with earth below, sky above, air between, and gods managing the forces that kept everything running. The created world was taking shape. The age of cosmic creation was ending, and the age of divine drama was beginning.

Alternative Origins: How Memphis and Hermopolis Saw the World Differently

The Heliopolis creation story—Atum on the mound, Shu and Tefnut, the Ennead—is the most famous version, but it is not the only one. Ancient Egypt wasn't one unified culture with a single official religion. Different cities had their own temples, favorite gods, and creation myths. These myths existed side by side, sometimes contradicting each other, sometimes mixing together, but rarely causing any serious conflict.

Egypt was huge. The distance from the Mediterranean coast to the First Cataract of the Nile was about six hundred miles. Communication was slow. Each major city developed its own religious center with its own priests who had their own interpretations of how everything began. And unlike later religions that demanded one true version of events, the Egyptians were comfortable with multiple truths existing at the same time.

The most important alternative creation myth came from Memphis, ancient Egypt's capital in the north. The Memphis version told a completely different story about creation, one that put thinking and speaking above physical acts.

In the Memphis version, creation started with Ptah, the craftsman god. Ptah didn't pop out of water or masturbate companions into being. Instead, he created the world through thought and words. Ptah imagined creation in his heart (which Egyptians thought was where you did your thinking), then spoke it into reality with his tongue. Thought became word, and word became reality.

This might sound familiar if you know the biblical creation story where God speaks the world into being. "Let there be light," and there was light. The Memphis version came first by over a thousand years and presented a surprisingly smart idea. Thinking comes before doing, words carry power, and creation is an intentional, planned act rather than a spontaneous or physical one.

The Shabaka Stone, a carved piece of basalt now in the British Museum, preserves this Memphis theology. It describes how Ptah conceived of every god, creature, and plant in his heart and then spoke their names to bring them into being. This was creation through intellect and language, not bodily fluids. The tongue that pronounced the names and the heart that conceived them were the true creative powers.

The Shabaka Stone.[*]

The Memphis texts even claim that Ptah created Atum and the Ennead through his thoughts and words. This was Memphis's way of saying they had the better creation story. Ptah was the ultimate creator, as everything else flowed from his intellectual act.

This kind of religious rivalry was normal in ancient Egypt. Each major city wanted its favorite deity to be supreme. The solution was usually blending—mixing gods together or creating rankings that let multiple claims be true. Ptah could be the first creator whose thoughts made Atum, who then physically created the Ennead. Everyone wins, sort of. The gods weren't competing for worshipers the way modern religions compete. They were just different aspects of the same cosmic truth.

The Memphis version also connected creation to kingship in interesting ways. Ptah's creative power through speech mirrored the pharaoh's power to make announcements that became reality. When the king said something, it happened. His word was literally law. This was Ptah's creative power working through the royal office. The Memphis priests weren't just describing how the universe began. They were explaining political authority and justifying why the pharaoh's commands had to be obeyed. If the pharaoh was using Ptah's creative speech, then disobeying the king meant opposing creation itself.

The other major alternative came from Hermopolis, a city in Middle Egypt. The Hermopolis version featured the Ogdoad—eight ancient deities who existed in the waters of Nu before creation started. If Heliopolis emphasized the one becoming many, and Memphis emphasized thought creating matter, Hermopolis emphasized the chaotic forces that had to exist before order emerged.

These eight gods came in four male-female pairs, each standing for an aspect of pre-creation chaos: Nu and Naunet (water), Huh and Hauhet (infinity), Kuk (or Kek) and Kauket (darkness), and Amun and Amaunet (hiddenness). Notice the pattern—each female name is just the male name with a feminine ending added. They weren't really individuals with distinct personalities. Think of them more like labeled forces, like "Darkness" and "Darkness-ness," "Water" and "Water-ness." The Egyptians were naming the basic ingredients that existed before the universe was organized enough to have actual gods with personalities.

These eight forces didn't sit down and plan creation. They didn't make decisions or have meetings. They just existed together in the primordial waters, and somehow, their presence created the first mound rising from the chaos. From that mound came either Ra or a cosmic egg that hatched Ra.

What makes the Hermopolis version interesting is its emphasis on the unknown and the hidden. Amun, whose name literally means "the hidden one," would eventually become one of Egypt's most powerful gods. During the New Kingdom, he merged with Ra to become Amun-Ra, king of the gods. The Hermopolis myth explained where Amun came from. He was one of the eight original forces, representing hiddenness itself. He was hidden because he existed before there was anything to see or be seen. He was mystery in its purest form.

The Ogdoad were sometimes depicted as frogs and serpents, which made sense to the Egyptians. Frogs appeared suddenly after the Nile's flood, seeming to pop up spontaneously from the mud. Serpents lived between worlds, sliding from water to land or from the civilized riverbank to the wild desert. Both creatures represented the boundary between order and chaos.

After the Ogdoad finished their work of accidentally creating the world, they supposedly died and were buried beneath Hermopolis. However, their presence in the earth kept things fertile.

A depiction of the Ogdoad.'

So why did Egyptians have multiple creation stories that contradicted each other? Two reasons.

First, politics. Each major city wanted its local god to be the most important. Memphis promoted Ptah. Heliopolis promoted Atum. Hermopolis promoted the Ogdoad. Having your god as the creator of everything brought prestige to your city, attracted pilgrims, and drew offerings and donations. It was good for business and civic pride.

Second—and this is the more interesting reason—Egyptians didn't think a person had to choose just one true story. They were perfectly comfortable with multiple stories being true at the same time. They were just describing the same basic event from different angles. The Heliopolis version focused on the physical process—things separating and dividing. The Memphis version focused on the mental aspect—thought and planning. The Hermopolis version focused on the raw materials—what had to exist before creation could even start.

This is hard for modern people to wrap their heads around because we're used to religions that demand one official version of events. But ancient Egyptians saw it differently. The universe was huge, complicated, and mysterious. Of course you'd need multiple stories to capture different parts of the truth. Using just one story would be like describing a building by only looking at it from one side. You'd miss important details.

A regular Egyptian could honor Ptah's creative intelligence, participate in festivals celebrating Ra's daily journey across the sky, and acknowledge that the Ogdoad existed before everything, all without feeling confused or contradictory. These weren't competing claims. They were complementary perspectives.

This flexibility ran through all of Egyptian religion. Gods could merge together when it made sense. Ra and Atum were sometimes the same being, sometimes separate. Amun absorbed Ra's solar aspects to become Amun-Ra. Gods could split apart again later if needed. Creation could start with Atum, Ptah, the Ogdoad, or all three in different ways. The goal wasn't to have one pure, consistent doctrine. The goal was to understand that the organized world emerged from chaos through divine power and that order had to be maintained through Ma'at (more on that later).

For the rest of this book, we'll mostly stick with the Heliopolis version because it has the most dramatic stories and vivid personalities. While everyday people might have known only the version told in their local temple, the priesthood and religious texts recorded all of them.

The universe was big enough to hold multiple true stories about how it began. And now that creation was complete, now that the world had structure and the gods had personalities and roles, the real drama could start. The Ennead had been assembled. The stage was set. What happened next would shape Egyptian civilization for three thousand years.

Chapter 2: The Drama of Osiris and Isis

The Golden Couple: Osiris as the First King of Egypt

After the Ennead organized the cosmos, the gods needed someone to actually rule it. That someone was Osiris, the firstborn son of Geb and Nut. Being born first mattered in Egyptian culture. The eldest inherited the throne, the property, and the authority. Osiris didn't have to fight for his position or prove himself worthy. He was king because he came out first on that stolen day outside the calendar.

And by all accounts, Osiris was good at ruling.

Before Osiris, there were no cities, farms, or temples rising along the Nile. Just scattered groups of people wandering the river valley, eating wild plants, hunting whatever animals they could catch, living day to day with no plan beyond survival. They had fire and basic tools, but they hadn't figured out how to shape the world around them. They were at the mercy of nature, not its masters.

The myths describe Osiris as Egypt's first pharaoh, the god who taught humans how to live civilized lives. He didn't arrive with armies or demand obedience through force. He came with knowledge and showed people a better way to live.

He showed them how to observe the Nile's cycle, how the river would swell every year at the same time, flooding the valley and depositing its load of rich black silt. When the water receded, the land was perfect for planting. Osiris gave humans seeds. He showed them how to prepare the soil, when to plant, how to tend the growing crops, and when to harvest.

Wheat and barley became staples. Bread and beer—the foundations of the Egyptian diet—came from these grains. Osiris personally demonstrated how to mill grain into flour, how to bake bread in clay ovens, and how to brew beer in large jars. These weren't just survival skills. They were the building blocks of civilization. You can't have cities without reliable food. You can't have specialization of labor when everyone's hunting their next meal. Agriculture changed everything.

He also showed them how to tend vines and make wine. Wine was sacred in Egypt; it was used in religious rituals and celebrations. The process of fermentation seemed magical. Grapes transformed into an intoxicating drink that could alter consciousness and bring people closer to the divine. Osiris revealed these secrets.

But Osiris gave humans more than farming techniques. He also brought Ma'at into human life.

Ma'at—cosmic order, balance, and truth—wasn't just an abstract principle. Osiris showed people how to live in harmony with it. Don't murder, as that creates chaos. Don't steal, as that breaks trust and community. Honor your agreements. Respect the gods through proper worship. Care for your family.

These principles would later appear in texts like the Book of the Dead as the Negative Confessions—declarations a dead person would make in the afterlife. "I have not killed. I have not stolen. I have not lied." However, Osiris didn't hand down commandments like a lawgiver. His very existence embodied these principles. He ruled justly, and Ma'at flowed from him naturally. When the king maintained Ma'at, society reflected that cosmic order. The Nile flooded. Crops grew. People lived in peace. It was all connected.

Osiris didn't stay in one place. He traveled throughout Egypt, teaching these skills to every community he encountered. And wherever he went, people loved him. The texts describe him as generous, patient, and wise. He didn't hoard knowledge or demand tribute. He freely shared everything he knew because he genuinely wanted humanity to thrive.

His physical appearance matched his character. Most depictions show Osiris with green or black skin, the colors of fertile earth and vegetation. He wore the white crown of Upper Egypt, symbolizing his kingship. He carried the crook and flail, the shepherd's tools that represented his role as caretaker of his people.

The Egyptians looked back on Osiris's reign as a golden age, not because life was easy—farming was hard work, and the Nile could be unpredictable—but because there was order and purpose. There was a sense that life had meaning beyond mere survival. People could plant crops knowing they'd reap the harvest. They could make plans for the future. They could build permanent homes instead of temporary shelters. This was Ma'at made manifest—the world working the way it should work.

Standing beside Osiris through all of this was Isis, his sister and wife. Egyptian gods regularly married their siblings, and Egyptian royalty later did the same to keep bloodlines pure and power consolidated. The marriage between Osiris and Isis wasn't about romance in the modern sense; it was more about maintaining cosmic balance through the union of complementary forces.

Isis was more than just Osiris's queen. She was a powerful goddess in her own right, eventually becoming one of the most important deities in the entire Egyptian pantheon. Her cult would spread far beyond Egypt, reaching Greece and Rome, and would last into the early centuries of the Common Era.

While Osiris taught practical skills, Isis mastered the supernatural. She knew spells and incantations that could heal sickness, protect against evil, and bend reality to her will. She understood the hidden names of things, which gave her power over them. In Egyptian magic, knowing something's true name meant you could control it. Names weren't just labels; they were the essence of what something was.

Isis dedicated herself to learning these names. She learned them through observation, study, and trickery when necessary. Later myths would describe how she extracted Ra's secret name through clever deception, gaining power over the sun god himself. At this point in the story, she was already recognized as the greatest magician among the gods, second only perhaps to Thoth in her knowledge of hidden things.

Together, Osiris and Isis represented ideal rulership. He brought order, agriculture, and law. She brought magic, wisdom, and protection. Where he was open and generous, she was clever and strategic. Where he ruled through inspiration, she ruled through knowledge. They complemented each other perfectly. They were two halves of a complete whole.

Their marriage wasn't just political or practical. The texts describe genuine affection between them. They chose each other and worked together willingly. In a world where gods often schemed against each other and marriages were arranged for political advantage, Osiris and Isis stood out as partners who actually wanted to be together.

Egypt prospered under their rule. The Nile reliably flooded each year. Crops grew in abundance. People had enough to eat, enough surplus to trade, and enough stability to develop arts, crafts, and culture. Villages grew into towns. Towns developed into cities. The foundations of Egyptian civilization were being laid.

This wasn't just good government. The Egyptians believed a righteous king kept the cosmos functioning properly. The pharaoh was the human link between heaven and earth. Osiris proved this principle. His just rule maintained Ma'at, which meant the Nile flooded, which in turn meant rich harvests, which in turn meant prosperous people.

But in this paradise, poison was growing. Set, Osiris's younger brother, watched everything with increasing resentment.

Set wasn't evil, not in the simple sense. He was the god of the desert, storms, violence, and chaos. These forces had their place in the natural order. The desert, harsh and deadly as it was, formed Egypt's natural borders and protected the Nile Valley from invaders. Storms brought destructive winds but also needed rain. Violence had its place in defending Ma'at against the forces of chaos. Set protected Ra's solar boat every night, spearing the chaos serpent Apep to ensure the sun would rise again.

Set was necessary. He was strong, fierce, and powerful. In many ways, he was more impressive than Osiris. Where Osiris was gentle and generous, Set was forceful and commanding. Where Osiris taught and persuaded, Set dominated and conquered. Set had raw power that Osiris lacked.

However, Set didn't have the throne.

The resentment ate at him. Why should Osiris get to be king just because he happened to be born first? Birth order was an accident. Power was real. Strength was real. And Set was stronger than Osiris. He would be better suited to rule through force and intimidation. He could make people obey through fear if necessary.

Instead, he had to watch his older brother receive all the glory, all the worship, and all the love. Osiris the Wise. Osiris the Just. Osiris the Generous. People sang songs about Osiris. They built shrines to Osiris. They blessed Osiris's name at every harvest.

Nobody sang songs about Set.

The myths don't usually give Set complex psychological depth. He wanted power and resented his brother. He felt cheated by fate. That was enough. In the Egyptian worldview, Set embodied the principle of disruption: the force that challenges order, breaks patterns, and introduces violence into peace. He was playing his cosmic role by opposing Osiris, even if he didn't think of it that way.

Set's jealousy grew and festered. Every time he saw Osiris celebrated, it burned a little hotter. Every time he heard people praise his brother's wisdom and justice, he thought about his own superior strength being wasted. Every time Isis looked at Osiris with love and admiration, Set felt the insult of being passed over.

Eventually, resentment turned to hatred. Hatred turned to murder.

Being a god of chaos and violence, Set didn't plan to challenge Osiris openly or honorably. He planned something treacherous, elaborate, and perfectly designed to destroy his brother while appearing innocent.

The stage was set—literally—for one of Egyptian mythology's most famous and brutal betrayals.

The Ultimate Betrayal: Set, the Seventy-two Conspirators, and the Chest

Set didn't act alone. Murdering a god-king required help, planning, and accomplices who could keep secrets. Set recruited seventy-two conspirators to help him kill Osiris.

Who were these seventy-two conspirators? The myths don't name them all. They were probably other gods and divine beings who resented Osiris for various reasons. Maybe they thought Set deserved the throne based on strength rather than birth order. Maybe they wanted positions of power in a new regime led by Set. Maybe they simply enjoyed chaos and wanted to see what would happen if the perfect king fell. Or maybe they feared Set's power and joined him rather than risk becoming his enemies.

Set gathered these allies in secret. He held private meetings, made promises, and extracted oaths. Everyone involved knew they were planning something that violated every rule of divine and social order. You didn't murder your own brother. You didn't murder the rightful king. You certainly didn't murder the god who embodied Ma'at itself. But Set convinced them all that it could be done, that it should be done, and that they'd benefit from doing it.

The plan itself was brilliant in its deception. Set didn't challenge Osiris to combat. He would probably lose or at least face public judgment. He also didn't stage a military coup; Osiris was beloved, and most gods would defend him. He didn't poison Osiris at a private meal, as that would be too suspicious and obvious.

Instead, Set threw a banquet.

This is the story as told in later accounts, particularly by the Greek-Egyptian writer Plutarch, who wrote over a thousand years after the height of Egyptian power. Earlier Egyptian sources don't give us specific details about a feast; they just tell us Osiris was murdered by Set. Instead, they focus more on what happened after. Plutarch's version became the most famous telling, adding dramatic details that made the story compelling to Greek audiences.

Banquets were sacred in Egyptian culture. They were times of abundance, celebration, and communal bonding between friends and family. Hosts and guests had mutual obligations. The host provided food, drink, entertainment, and safety. Guests showed respect, brought gifts, and participated in the joy. Violence at a feast violated every social and cosmic law. It was unthinkable.

Set was counting on that. He used cultural trust as his weapon.

He sent invitations throughout the divine realm. They were to come celebrate. Bring their best stories and enjoy the finest food and wine Egypt has to offer. Everyone was invited, including Osiris.

Osiris received the invitation and accepted immediately. Why wouldn't he? Set was his brother. It seemed as if Set had finally accepted his role and was planning to finally honor his elder brother properly.

Isis had doubts. She was clever, suspicious, and magically attuned to threats. She probably sensed something was wrong. But what could she say? You can't refuse your own brother's feast invitation without serious cause. And if Set was genuinely trying to reconcile, refusing would create the very division they wanted to avoid.

So, Osiris went. The banquet was magnificent. Set had spared no expense. The great hall blazed with torchlight. Tables overflowed with bread, roasted meat, fruits, vegetables, and cakes dripping with honey. Wine flowed freely. It was strong enough to blur the edges of worry and loosen tongues into laughter.

Musicians played harps, flutes, and drums. Dancers performed. Servants circulated the room with fresh cups of wine. The seventy-two conspirators mingled with innocent guests, their smiles hiding their deadly knowledge. Set played the perfect host. He was welcoming, generous, and entertaining. He told jokes. He honored Osiris with toasts praising his brother's wisdom and justice. He seemed genuinely happy.

The feast went on for hours. Everyone ate and drank. Tensions that might have existed melted away in the warm glow of wine and celebration.

Then Set unveiled his surprise.

Servants carried in an enormous chest and set it in the center of the hall. Everyone turned to look. The chest was extraordinary, a work of art that drew gasps of admiration. It was made from precious cedar wood, inlaid with gold and jewels, and carved with intricate designs of stars and sacred symbols. The torchlight made the gold gleam and the gems sparkle. It was the most beautiful object most of the gods had ever seen.

Set stood and announced that this treasure would be a gift, but it would not be given freely—that would be too simple. The chest would go to whoever fit inside it perfectly.

This didn't seem strange to the guests. The Egyptians loved games and contests at celebrations. Senet, wrestling, archery, riddles—entertainment was part of any good feast. And a chest that fits you perfectly would be an amazing possession. Chests stored valuables, clothes, important documents, and magical amulets. A custom-fit chest lined with precious materials would be both practical and luxurious.

Guests started volunteering. One after another, they climbed into the chest to try their luck.

The first guest was too tall. His feet stuck out over the edge. Everyone laughed.

The next was too wide. She couldn't fit her shoulders through the opening. More laughter.

Someone else was too short. He rattled around inside with space to spare. The guests cheered and jeered good-naturedly as person after person tried and failed to fit the chest perfectly.

Set's seventy-two conspirators also tried, maintaining the pretense. They already knew the chest wasn't made for them. They climbed in, didn't fit, and climbed out with exaggerated disappointment. All part of the show.

Finally, Set turned to Osiris. "Brother, you haven't tried. Surely the king should test this magnificent chest. Perhaps it was made for you."

Everyone turned to Osiris. They clapped and called out their encouragement. It was all in good fun. It was harmless entertainment.

Osiris smiled. He'd watched everyone else fail. He was probably curious to see if he'd fit any better. He stepped forward, climbed into the chest, and lay down inside it.

It fit perfectly.

The crowd cheered. Osiris had won the contest. The beautiful chest was his. He started to sit up, ready to claim his prize and accept congratulations.

Then Set gave the signal.

The seventy-two conspirators moved as one. They rushed forward from all sides of the hall. Before Osiris could react and before any of the innocent guests understood what was happening, the conspirators slammed the lid shut.

Osiris was trapped inside.

They worked with practiced speed. Some held the lid down while Osiris pounded from within, his muffled shouts barely audible. Others produced hammers and nails—tools they'd hidden beforehand. They nailed the lid shut. Long bronze nails were driven through the rim of the lid into the body of the chest, sealing it completely.

Osiris was beating against the lid from inside. The chest shook from his efforts. The gods could hear his voice calling for help, for Isis, for anyone to stop this.

But the conspirators weren't finished. They poured molten lead over the seams. The hot metal flowed into every gap, crack, and tiny opening. It cooled instantly on contact with the wood, creating an airtight seal. No water could get in. No air could get in. Nothing could get in.

And nothing could get out.

The banquet hall erupted in chaos. Innocent guests screamed and fled. Some tried to intervene, but the conspirators formed a wall around the sealed chest.

Osiris was suffocating inside the chest. The Egyptian texts don't dwell on his final moments—the panic of being sealed in complete darkness, the realization of betrayal, the desperate gasps as the air ran out. But it must have been horrific. Here was a god dying like a trapped animal, murdered by his own brother, and betrayed at a feast held in his honor. This was a social violation on every possible level.

Osiris died inside the chest. The firstborn son of Geb and Nut, the king who brought civilization to Egypt, the god who embodied order and justice, lay dead, sealed in what had looked like a gift but was actually a custom-built coffin.

Set stood over the sealed chest, triumphant. He'd done it. His brother was dead, and his hands were technically clean. The conspirators had done the physical work. Set had just thrown a party and offered a prize. He had plausible deniability if anyone even dared to question him.

But Set wasn't finished. Killing Osiris wasn't enough. He needed the body gone. If Osiris's body remained in Egypt, Isis might find a way to use her magic on it. Set had heard the stories about Isis's power. She knew spells that could heal, restore, and even reverse death under the right circumstances.

Set ordered his conspirators to carry the sealed chest to the Nile. They hauled it through the night to the riverbank and threw it into the water.

The Nile was Egypt's lifeline, but it was also Egypt's highway. Everything that entered the river traveled north toward the Mediterranean Sea. Set expected the heavy chest would sink in the deep water or get lost in the marshes of the delta. Maybe it would wash out to sea and sink in the Mediterranean. Either way, Osiris would be gone forever.

He was wrong about what would happen next.

The chest didn't sink. Whether because of the wood's buoyancy, divine intervention, or simple chance, the sealed chest floated. The current caught it and carried it downstream, past sleeping villages, past fields and temples, past everything Osiris had built and taught and cherished.

The chest traveled through the night, through the next day, and for days after that. It passed the entire length of the Nile, moving north. It reached the delta and passed through the marshes where papyrus grew thick. It entered the Mediterranean Sea.

And it kept floating.

The current carried it along the coast, past Egypt's borders. It drifted north and east until it reached Byblos, a Phoenician city in what's now modern Lebanon, hundreds of miles from Egypt.

At Byblos, waves pushed the chest toward shore. It washed up on a beach near a tamarisk tree growing at the water's edge.

What happened next was the natural response of the divine power still resident in Osiris's body. The tamarisk tree began to grow. This was not the normal slow growth of trees; instead, it rapidly grew. The tree's roots spread. Its trunk thickened. It grew around the chest that had washed up beneath it, incorporating the sealed coffin into its own wood.

The chest became part of the tree. Osiris's body was now hidden inside the trunk of a massive tamarisk, sealed in wood within wood, invisible to anyone who didn't know to look for it.

The tree grew so large and so beautiful that it attracted attention. The king of Byblos heard about this magnificent tamarisk and came to see it himself. He ordered it cut down. He wanted it as a support beam for the roof of his throne room. His servants cut the tree, trimmed it, and installed it in the palace.

They never noticed the seam in the wood. They never suspected that inside this pillar, sealed in a chest sealed in wood, lay the murdered god-king of Egypt.

Meanwhile, back in Egypt, Set took the throne. The witnesses at the feast knew what had happened, but Set's terrifying power kept them silent. Without Osiris's body and with no one brave enough to testify, Set ruled.

However, one person knew the truth. One person felt Osiris's death like a knife in her own heart. One person would never stop searching, never stop fighting, and never accept Set's lies.

The Quest of Isis: Magic, Mourning, and the Search for the Pieces

Isis knew her husband was dead the moment it happened. She didn't need messengers or witnesses. She didn't need to see the sealed chest or watch Set's triumph. She felt it. The bond between them went deeper than marriage. They were cosmic partners, two halves of divine order working in perfect harmony. When Osiris died, Isis felt the world fracture. Ma'at cracked, and the balance tilted.

The moment his last breath left his body, Isis felt a piece of herself die with him.

She also knew Set was responsible. Whispers spread through the divine realm. There had been a banquet. A chest. Osiris disappeared, and now Set sat on the throne. The story didn't require genius to decipher. And Isis wasn't just intelligent—she was the greatest magician among the gods. She had ways of learning what others tried to hide.

Her grief was immense and public. Egyptian texts describe Isis and her sister Nephthys, the wife of Set, wailing in mourning that shook the heavens. Their cries echoed across Egypt, a sound that every widow, every mother who lost a child, and every sister who buried a brother would later imitate. The goddesses' mourning became the template for human grief.

And yes, Set's own wife mourned with Isis. Nephthys sided with Isis, not her husband. She had never supported Set's violence or his coup. When the choice came between her violent husband and her sister, she chose her sister without hesitation. The two goddesses mourned together, their voices blending in the traditional call-and-response wails that Egyptian women would sing at funerals for thousands of years afterward.

But Isis didn't just mourn. She searched.

She couldn't just sit and weep while her husband's body drifted somewhere unknown. Osiris deserved a proper burial. He deserved the rituals that would allow his soul to survive in the afterlife. Without his body, without mummification, and without the proper spells and ceremonies, Osiris would face oblivion. This was known as true death, the second death that meant the complete annihilation of the soul.

Isis refused to let that happen. So, she transformed herself. Many goddesses could shift their shapes, and Isis used this power to travel incognito. Sometimes she appeared as an old woman. Sometimes she appeared as a common laborer or a bird. She moved through Egypt asking everyone she met the same question: Have you seen a chest floating in the Nile?

Most people hadn't seen anything. However, children playing by the river had better memories than adults focused on daily work. They'd seen a beautiful chest, gleaming in the sunlight, float by, carried by the current. They told Isis which direction it had gone.

She followed the trail north, asking at every village along the Nile. At each town, she found someone who remembered seeing the chest. It became a breadcrumb trail leading downstream toward the sea.

The search exhausted her. Days became weeks. She traveled hundreds of miles, sleeping in poor conditions and eating whatever she could find. She never stopped for long. The other gods watched her quest with a mixture of pity and admiration. Some helped with information. Others stayed silent, afraid of Set's wrath.

The trail eventually led Isis out of Egypt entirely. The chest had left the Nile and entered the Mediterranean. It had floated beyond Egyptian territory. But Isis didn't care about boundaries. Her husband's body was out there somewhere, and she would find it even if she had to search every coastline in the world.

Divine intuition and fragments of information led her to Byblos. She arrived at the Phoenician city and began asking questions. Nobody knew about a chest, but everyone talked about the amazing tamarisk tree that had grown so fast and so large that the king had made it into a pillar for his palace.

Something about this resonated with Isis. She felt drawn to the palace, pulled by the same connection that had let her feel Osiris's death. He was here, close by. She knew it.

But she couldn't just march into the foreign king's palace and announce herself as an Egyptian goddess demanding to search the building. That would cause diplomatic problems, possibly even violence. So Isis used cunning instead of power.

She disguised herself as an old woman. She hung around the palace, waiting for an opportunity. Eventually, she encountered the queen's servants by a well. They were drawing water, chatting, and complaining about their work. Isis struck up a conversation.

She was charming and kind. She offered to braid one servant's hair, which she did so beautifully. Word of her skill reached the queen herself, who sent for this talented old woman. The queen asked Isis if she could serve in the palace. The queen's infant son needed a nursemaid, and this woman seemed gentle and skilled.

Isis accepted the position. She became the royal nursemaid, tending the prince during the day. She lived in the palace and had access to every room, including the throne room with its magnificent pillar. She felt Osiris's presence there more strongly. She was sure that the pillar held him.

But she couldn't just tear apart the king's structural support. She had to wait and bide her time. And while she waited, she decided to do something extraordinary for the baby she was tending.

Isis wanted to make the child immortal. The texts don't fully explain why. Maybe it was gratitude to the foreign queen who unknowingly housed her husband's body. Maybe it was payment for being allowed to stay in the palace. Maybe Isis, grieving her own dead husband and unable to save him, wanted to save this child from ever experiencing death.

Each night, after the palace slept, Isis performed the ritual. She placed the baby in the hearth fire, not to harm him but to purify him. Divine flames burned differently from ordinary fire. They could burn away mortality itself, transforming a human child into an immortal being. But the process required time. Night after night, the baby had to be placed in the flames, gradually burning away the mortal parts until only the immortal essence remained.

Night after night, Isis performed the ritual. The baby never cried because the fire never harmed him.

However, one night, the queen woke up. Maybe she heard a sound, or maybe maternal instinct pulled her from sleep. She came to check on her son and found a terrifying sight: the old nursemaid holding her baby over roaring flames.

The queen screamed. Her shriek shattered the night. Guards came running. The king burst into the room. They saw the baby in the fire and assumed a murder was happening.

Isis had to stop the ritual immediately. She pulled the child from the flames. He was unharmed but still mortal. The transformation wasn't complete. The boy would live a normal human lifespan now, aging and eventually dying like everyone else.

The queen sobbed, reaching for her child. The king shouted for guards to seize the murderous nursemaid. The entire palace erupted in chaos and fury.

Isis had no choice. She revealed herself.

The disguise fell away. The humble old woman transformed into the full radiance of the goddess Isis. Divine power blazed from her, light filling the room. Everyone in the room fell to their knees, terrified and awed.

The king and queen were shaking. A goddess had been living in their palace, serving them. They begged for forgiveness, though they didn't know what they'd done wrong. They pleaded for their lives and their son's life.

Isis wasn't angry. She explained everything. The baby was safe, although the ritual had been interrupted, so he'd remain mortal. She meant no threat to the royal family.

What she did need was the pillar. She told them the truth about her husband and how that pillar held his body. She needed that chest back.

The king didn't hesitate. He immediately called for craftsmen. Work began that very night, despite the late hour. They couldn't leave a goddess waiting. Using careful tools, the craftsmen cut into the massive pillar. They worked slowly, precisely, finding the seam in the wood where the chest had been incorporated. They extracted the sealed chest from the pillar without damaging it, then presented it to Isis.

Inside this sealed box was her husband's body. She could feel his presence stronger than ever. He was dead, but he was here. She had finally found him.

The king and queen offered her anything else she wanted. Gold, jewels, ships, soldiers—whatever an Egyptian goddess might desire. Isis asked only for the remains of the pillar, the wood that had housed her husband. She blessed it with powerful magic, making it a sacred relic. The wood would bring good fortune and divine protection to Byblos. The city would prosper because it had unknowingly sheltered a god.

Then Isis took the chest and left. She traveled back to Egypt with her precious cargo, guarding it every moment of the journey. She arrived in the Nile Delta and hid the chest in the papyrus marshes—thick swamps where reeds grew taller than a person, where birds nested and crocodiles lurked. It was a place where few humans ever ventured.

This was the safest place she knew. She could hide here and work in secret. She needed time to open the chest properly and to prepare the magic that might, just might, bring him back. She also needed time to grieve privately, without the weight of divine politics and Set's spies watching her every move.

But time was the one thing she didn't have.

Set found out. Someone saw her. Someone told him. Or perhaps he'd been actively searching, using his own magic to scry for Osiris's body. However it happened, Set learned that Isis had recovered the chest and hidden it in the delta marshes.

Set hunted for it. He scoured the papyrus swamps, searching for any sign of the chest. Eventually, he found it.

Finding Osiris's body wasn't enough. Isis had brought it back once. Her magic was powerful. Who knew what she might be able to do with an intact corpse? Maybe she had spells that could revive him. Maybe she could animate his body like a puppet. Maybe Osiris could come back and challenge Set's claim to the throne.

Set couldn't allow any of that. He needed to make absolutely certain that Osiris could never return, that Isis's magic would be useless, and that his brother stayed dead forever.

So Set opened the chest, pulled out Osiris's preserved body, and tore it into pieces.

The exact number varies between sources. The earliest versions typically say fourteen pieces—a number connected to the lunar cycle and the waning of the moon. Later accounts, especially from the Ptolemaic period when Greeks ruled Egypt, use forty-two pieces—one for each of the forty-two nomes, the administrative districts of Egypt.

Set used a knife. He cut with divine strength, severing the limbs from the torso, separating the head from the body, and removing organs, dismembering thoroughly and methodically.

Then Set traveled the length of Egypt, throwing the pieces far apart. A leg in the far south. An arm in the north. The head somewhere else. Organs scattered randomly. He distributed the pieces deliberately, making sure they'd be impossible to find.

This was Set's greatest crime. Killing Osiris was murder. Dismembering him was desecration. The Egyptians believed that the body needed to be intact for the soul to survive in the afterlife. No body meant no afterlife. Scattered pieces meant eternal oblivion.

Set threw the last piece into the Nile and walked away satisfied. Osiris was truly gone now. Even Isis, with all her magic, couldn't bring back a person who existed in forty-two pieces spread across hundreds of miles.

He underestimated Isis.

When she discovered what Set had done, her grief turned to grim determination. She would find every piece, no matter how long it took, no matter how far she had to travel. She would make her husband whole again.

She enlisted her sister Nephthys. Together, the two goddesses began the second search. They walked the entire length of Egypt, from the Mediterranean coast to the southern cataracts. They asked priests at every temple. They questioned farmers in every field. They searched along riverbanks, in deserts, in marshes, and in cities.

And slowly, piece by piece, they found him.

The myths say that wherever they found a piece of Osiris, they buried it temporarily and built a shrine to mark the spot. This explained why so many temples across Egypt claimed to house relics of Osiris.

The search took a long time, but Isis never stopped. She found his arms. His legs. His torso. His head. His organs. One by one, she collected the scattered pieces of her husband.

But there was one piece Isis couldn't recover: Osiris's phallus.

Set had thrown it into the Nile, and a fish had eaten it. Some texts specify that it was the *Oxyrhynchus* fish, a Nile perch that became sacred afterward because it had consumed part of a god.

This created a serious problem. Osiris couldn't be whole without all his parts. Plus, Isis had plans that required Osiris to be anatomically complete.

So, she did what no one but the greatest magician could do. She created a replacement. Using divine magic, gold from Egypt's mines, and wax from sacred bees, Isis fashioned an artificial phallus. She shaped it carefully, imbuing it with magic to make it functional. She then attached it to Osiris's reassembled body.

Through her power, she made the replacement as real as the original. Now Osiris's body was complete again. Forty-one original pieces plus one magical replacement. All that remained was to properly preserve the body and perform the rituals that might bring him back.

The First Mummy: Anubis and the Birth of the Afterlife

Anubis appeared when Isis needed him most. The jackal-headed god materialized in the papyrus marshes where Isis had laid out Osiris's reassembled body. Where he came from in this moment depends on which version of the myth you follow. Some texts say Anubis was Osiris's own son by Nephthys, conceived in a complicated affair that happened before the murder. Other versions portray him as a separate god who appeared only when death required his expertise. Either way, Anubis was the god of death and embalming, and he knew exactly what to do with a body.

Anubis brought knowledge that no one else possessed. He understood the secrets of preservation, the techniques that would keep a body intact for eternity. The Egyptians had noticed that bodies left in the desert sand dried out and stayed preserved for years, sometimes decades. Moisture made bodies rot. Dryness preserved them. Anubis supposedly took this natural phenomenon and transformed it into a divine ritual.

The Osiris myth itself focuses on Anubis "binding the members" and "making the god whole," using magic and divine knowledge to restore Osiris's dismembered body. The detailed embalming techniques described here—the brain hooks, the natron, the forty-day drying period— come from actual Egyptian mortuary practices that developed over centuries. Priests who embalmed real bodies saw themselves as following the pattern Anubis established with Osiris.

The process looked something like this. First, Anubis washed Osiris's reassembled body with wine and water from the Nile. This cleansing removed physical impurities and spiritually prepared the body for transformation. The washing was a ritual purification, marking the transition from corrupted flesh to sacred vessel.

Then came the difficult part. Anubis used a bronze hook to extract Osiris's brain through the nose. The Egyptians didn't think the brain was particularly important—they believed thought and emotion resided in the heart—so the brain could be discarded. Anubis pulled it out in pieces and threw it away.

Next, he made an incision in Osiris's left side. Through this opening, he removed the internal organs—the lungs, liver, stomach, and intestines. These organs would quickly decay if left inside the body, so they had to be removed. However, they weren't discarded. They were important, so they'd be preserved separately.

The heart stayed in the body. It was the seat of intelligence, memory, and moral character. In the judgment one faces in the afterlife, the heart would be weighed against the feather of Ma'at. Without your heart, you couldn't be judged. Without judgment, you couldn't enter the afterlife. The heart had to remain.

Anubis washed the removed organs and packed them in natron, a natural salt mined from dried lake beds. The natron would dry out the organs just like it would dry out the body. Later, these preserved organs would be placed in special jars, each protected by one of the four sons of Horus. But that innovation came later. For now, Anubis simply preserved them.

Then he packed Osiris's entire body cavity with natron. He covered the body with more natron, creating a pile of salt completely encasing the corpse. And then he waited.

The texts are very specific: the body had to remain in natron for forty days. During this time, the salt drew out all the moisture from the tissues. The body dried out completely, becoming leathery and rigid, but it wouldn't decay. Decay required moisture.

After forty days, Anubis removed the natron. He washed the body again, this time with oils and perfumes. The dried skin absorbed these aromatic substances, which had preservative properties and made the body smell pleasant instead of like death.

Now came the wrapping. Anubis had strips of linen, hundreds of yards of cloth torn into long ribbons. He began wrapping Osiris's body, starting with the fingers and toes. Each digit was wrapped individually. Then the hands, the feet, and the limbs. Layer upon layer of linen, each strip was carefully placed, each layer adding protection.

Between the layers, Anubis placed amulets, magical objects that would protect Osiris in the afterlife. A scarab over the heart ensured it wouldn't testify against him in judgment. The djed pillar was for stability. Dozens of amulets, each with its own protective purpose, were all hidden in the wrappings.

The wrapping took thirty days. Every part of the body had to be covered properly. The final layers went around the entire body, binding it into a human-shaped package. The arms were crossed over the chest. The legs were placed together. The whole body was enclosed in linen.

This was the first mummy. The word "mummy" comes from the Arabic word for bitumen, a tar-like substance, because later mummies looked so dark that people thought they'd been dipped in tar. However, the darkness came from the oils and resins used in preservation, not from bitumen. Anubis had created something new—a preserved body that could last thousands of years.

But physical preservation wasn't enough. The body was sealed, unable to eat, drink, breathe, or speak. The senses were closed. The spirit couldn't interact with the world. This is where the Opening of the Mouth ceremony became essential.

Anubis performed this ritual using special tools. He touched Osiris's mouth with an adze, a copper blade used in carpentry. He touched the eyes, the nose, and the ears. Each touch was accompanied by spells and sacred words that activated the sealed senses.

The mouth opened (in a symbolic sense, not physically). Now Osiris could eat the offerings brought to him. He could speak the spells he'd need in the afterlife. He could breathe, even though he didn't need air anymore.

The eyes opened as well. Now Osiris could see the world of the living and the world of the dead. He could navigate the underworld. He could witness the offerings placed at his shrine.

The ears opened. Now Osiris could hear prayers, listen to his family mourning, and hear the sounds of the afterlife.

With the Opening of the Mouth ceremony complete, Osiris was ready. His body was preserved. His senses were restored. But he was still dead. The mummification process had prepared him for eternity, but it hadn't brought him back to life.

That required Isis's magic.

Throughout Anubis's work, Isis had been preparing her own spells. She'd watched and learned the embalming techniques, committing every detail to memory. But she was also gathering magical power, preparing for the most difficult spell she'd ever attempt—bringing the dead back to life.

The Egyptian texts describe what happened next in poetic language. Isis transformed into a kite, a bird of prey. She spread her wings and flew above Osiris's mummified body, hovering in the air. Some versions say she landed directly on the body, joining with him in bird form. Others describe her beating her wings rapidly, creating a magical wind that stirred the lifeless form below.

She spoke spells, words of power passed down from the first gods, words that commanded life and death, words that even Ra might not know. Her voice filled the marsh. Her magic filled the air. The wings beat faster.

Osiris stirred. His spirit had returned. Divine breath entered his lungs, and his eyes opened behind the linen wrappings.

And in those moments, Isis conceived a child with Osiris.

The texts describe this as miraculous, a conception that defied normal biology. Isis, in the form of a bird, hovered over Osiris's mummified body. Osiris was technically still dead but briefly animated by his wife's magic. Through divine will and magical power, Isis became pregnant.

This wasn't about physical pleasure or romance. This was about ensuring justice. Osiris needed an heir. Someone had to avenge his murder and reclaim the throne from Set. The child conceived in this impossible moment would be that avenger.

Isis copulating with Osiris.[5]

The child would be Horus—not Horus the Elder, the sky god who was part of the Ennead, but Horus the Younger.

With the conception complete, Osiris's brief return to life ended. His spirit left his body again. But this time, he didn't die completely. He didn't fade into nothingness. Instead, he descended into the underworld, the Duat, to become its ruler.

Osiris had a new role. He was no longer the god of living kings and agriculture. He became the god of dead kings and the afterlife. He left the land of the living permanently, but he didn't cease to exist. He became king of another realm entirely, although he was still connected to the earth. His death and return mirrored the cycle of planting and harvest, and he remained a powerful symbol of rebirth and fertility.

This transformation was revolutionary for the Egyptian religion. Before Osiris's death and resurrection, there was no clear afterlife in Egyptian creation myths. The stories talk about gods creating the world, organizing the cosmos, and establishing order, but they don't explain what happens to humans after death. Osiris's journey created the template for everyone who would die after him.

Osiris died violently through betrayal. His body was destroyed. But through love, proper burial practices, and magic, he achieved eternal life in a transformed state. He proved that death wasn't the end. It was a transition. A journey from one form of existence to another. If you died properly, if your body was preserved properly, if the right rituals were performed, and if your heart was pure enough to pass judgment, you, too, could live forever in a transformed state.

Every Egyptian who died would hope to "become Osiris." They'd hope their family would mourn as Isis had mourned. They'd hope their body would be mummified like Anubis mummified Osiris. They'd hope magical spells would restore their senses like the Opening of the Mouth restored Osiris's. And they'd hope to be judged worthy to live forever in the Field of Reeds, just like Osiris ruled forever in the Duat.

But Osiris's story is not finished yet. Osiris was in the underworld. Isis had conceived Horus. And Set still sat on the throne, ruling Egypt through force and fear, unaware that his brother's son was about to be born, a son who would grow up knowing only one purpose: revenge.

The drama is about to shift from murder and resurrection to something even more intense: a war for the throne of Egypt.

Chapter 3: Horus vs. Set: The Great Conflict

A Son's Revenge: The Birth and Hidden Childhood of Horus

Isis was pregnant with Osiris's child, conceived in that impossible moment between death and transformation. But she couldn't let anyone know, especially not Set. Set had murdered his brother, torn his body into pieces, and taken the throne through violence. If he discovered that Osiris had an heir, he'd hunt that child down and kill it before it could grow strong enough to challenge him.

So Isis hid.

She fled to the papyrus marshes of the Nile Delta, the same swamps where she'd hidden Osiris's chest before Set found it. The delta was vast, a maze of waterways and reed beds where crocodiles lurked and birds nested. It was dangerous territory, but that danger provided protection. Few people ventured deep into the marshes. Set's spies would have trouble finding her there.

The texts say Isis gave birth at a place called Khemmis, also known as Akhbity, somewhere in the delta marshes. The myths don't specify the exact location, though. She gave birth alone. No midwife attended her. No family surrounded her. It was just the goddess and her newborn son, hidden among the reeds while Set ruled Egypt from Osiris's stolen throne.

She named him Horus, Heru in Egyptian, meaning "the Distant One" or "the One on High." Horus would become the template for every pharaoh who ruled Egypt. Every king was the "Living Horus," the earthly embodiment of this god.

But right now, Horus was just a vulnerable infant. Gods could die. Osiris had proven that. Divine children could be killed before they reached their power. Isis knew she had to keep Horus hidden until he was strong enough to face Set.

She raised him in the marshes. She taught him to be silent and still when danger approached. Nephthys helped her too. Set's own wife had sided with her sister from the beginning. Some traditions say Nephthys visited the marshes to bring food and supplies, helping protect the young god during his early years. Isis taught Horus about his father, about what Set had done, and about his destiny to reclaim the throne.

But even with magical protection, the marshes were dangerous. One story tells how a scorpion stung young Horus. The venom spread quickly. He would have died, but Isis called out for help. Ra heard her cry from his boat in the sky and sent Thoth down to heal the child. Thoth knew spells that could counter any poison. He spoke the words, and the venom left Horus's body.

Horus grew up knowing one thing above all others: Set had murdered his father. He had stolen the throne and ruled Egypt through violence and fear. And Horus, as Osiris's legitimate heir, had the right and the duty to take that throne back.

Isis trained him. She taught him combat, magic, and strategy. She told him stories of Osiris's golden age, when Egypt prospered under a just rule. She described Ma'at and how Set's reign violated every principle of cosmic order. She explained that when Horus claimed the throne, he wouldn't just be taking power for himself. He'd be restoring Ma'at, bringing balance back to a world Set had broken.

Horus grew into a strong young god. He was handsome, fierce, and skilled in battle. Artists would later depict him with a falcon's head, like his distant relative Horus the Elder, because the falcon represented kingship and the sky.

Detail of Horus's face from the 12th century BCE.[6]

When Horus reached maturity, Isis decided it was time. She couldn't keep him hidden in the marshes forever. Set's illegitimate rule had lasted long enough. Horus was ready to challenge his uncle for the throne of Egypt.

However, she didn't want Horus to just attack Set directly. That would be civil war, god fighting god in open combat. Egypt would be torn apart. It would be better to bring the dispute before the divine council. The gods had ways of resolving conflicts between their own. Let the Ennead debate and decide who deserved the throne: Horus, the rightful heir, or Set, the powerful usurper.

The Divine Struggle: Ra's Indecision

The Ennead convened to hear the case. These were the great gods—Ra (or Ra-Atum since Ra and Atum were often treated as the same being), Shu, Tefnut, Geb, Nut, and others who had authority to judge such matters. They met in a great hall called the "Broad Hall," somewhere in the divine realm, to decide who should rule Egypt.

This wasn't a modern courtroom with lawyers and legal procedures. This was more like a family council or a meeting of tribal elders to settle a dispute between relatives. The gods argued, debated, took sides, changed their minds, and sometimes just bickered like any family dealing with internal conflict. The "trial" was really a divine struggle for dominance, with Horus and Set each trying to prove they deserved the throne.

Horus stood before them and made his claim. He was Osiris's son. By the laws of inheritance, the throne passed from father to eldest son. Osiris had been murdered, but that murder didn't erase Horus's birthright. He was the legitimate king. The throne was his by every principle of law and justice.

Most of the gods agreed. The case seemed clear. Geb, Horus's grandfather, particularly supported him.

Thoth, the god of wisdom and writing, sided with Horus as well. Thoth valued law and proper procedure. Shu and the other gods of the younger generation favored Horus. His cause was just. Ma'at demanded his victory.

But Set had his own argument, and it resonated with at least one very important god. Set stood before the tribunal, powerful, intimidating, and unashamed. Yes, he'd taken the throne by force. Yes, he'd killed Osiris. But power mattered. Strength mattered. He defended Ra's solar boat every single night, spearing Apep to ensure the sun would rise. Could Horus do that? Set was the strongest of the gods, the only one with enough raw power and ferocity to face down the chaos serpent night after night. Egypt needed a strong king to defend it from threats. Birth order was arbitrary. Power was real.

This argument swayed Ra. The sun god valued strength, and the story implies he was concerned about Set's role in defending the solar boat from Apep each night. If Set lost the throne and felt dishonored, would he still defend Ra's journey through the underworld? The text suggests Ra was reluctant to alienate his strongest defender, though his exact reasoning isn't spelled out explicitly.

Regardless of the reason, Ra hesitated. He suggested they hear more arguments, consider all perspectives, and take their time with such an important matter.

The other gods were frustrated. The case was obvious. Horus was the rightful king. But Ra outranked them. If Ra wouldn't decide, they couldn't force a verdict without causing a crisis.

Some gods openly criticized Ra's hesitation. The texts record that one god, Bebon, a minor deity, actually insulted Ra to his face, saying Ra's shrine was empty, meaning Ra had no real power or authority anymore. Ra was so offended that he went to his tent and lay down, refusing to participate in the proceedings.

The divine council was paralyzed without Ra. The gods sent Hathor, Ra's daughter, to cheer him up. She went to his tent and exposed herself to him, lifting her dress to show him her genitals. This made Ra laugh, breaking his sullen mood. He returned to the tribunal, and the proceedings continued.

This episode comes from the Chester Beatty Papyrus version of the story. It's one of those moments that shows how human-like Egyptian gods could be. They sulked, laughed at crude humor, and acted like family members having messy disputes. The Egyptians saw nothing shameful in this. Hathor's shocking gesture broke the tension and reminded Ra not to take himself too seriously.

The tribunal dragged on for years, then for decades. According to the text called *The Contendings of Horus and Set*, there were eighty years of legal arguments, debates, tricks, and delays while Set sat on the throne and Horus waited for justice.

Finally, the goddess Neith, who was older than most of the other gods, was asked to give her opinion. Neith was known for her wisdom and fair judgment. Surely she could resolve this.

Neith said Horus should have the throne. By every principle of justice and law, Osiris's son should inherit his father's position. But she suggested compensation for Set to make the verdict easier to accept. The gods should give Set double his current possessions. Let him have two foreign goddesses as wives, Anat and Astarte, warrior goddesses from Syria, to increase his honor and status. Let him keep his pride and power even while surrendering the throne.

Ra, however, objected. He complained that Horus was too young and inexperienced to rule, despite Horus being fully grown. The other gods started to suspect Ra was stalling deliberately. He needed Set to defend his boat, and he didn't want to anger his defender. But he also couldn't openly side with a murderer against legitimate justice. So he delayed, hoping something would resolve the situation without forcing him to choose.

Isis watched all of this with growing anger. The case was clear, but Ra's cowardice and favoritism toward Set were preventing justice. She decided to take matters into her own hands.

Using her magical powers, Isis transformed herself into a beautiful young woman. She put on jewelry and fine clothes and waited outside the hall where the gods deliberated. She caught Set alone. He didn't recognize her in her disguise.

She told him a sob story. She was a widow, she said, weeping. Her husband had been a cattle herder who died, leaving their son as heir to his cattle and property. But a stranger, an outsider with no family connection, had come and taken everything. He'd driven her son out of his own inheritance, claiming that because he was stronger and armed with a staff, the property should go to him instead of the legitimate heir.

Wasn't this unjust? Shouldn't the son inherit his father's property? Shouldn't the rightful heir receive what belonged to him by law?

Set, not recognizing the trap, responded with genuine indignation. Of course that was unjust. The son should inherit his father's property. A stranger had no right to steal what belonged to the legitimate heir just because he had a weapon. That violated every principle of law and inheritance. The widow's son should receive his father's cattle.

Isis immediately transformed back into her true form, revealing herself. Set had just condemned himself with his own words. She then turned into a bird and flew up into a tree, calling down to Set that his own mouth had judged him. The gods who witnessed this were delighted. Set had trapped himself through his own logic. His own sense of justice, at least when it came to other people's inheritance disputes, proved that Horus deserved the throne.

Set was furious. He'd been tricked by magic and clever words. This wasn't fair, nor was it a real debate. He appealed to Ra, demanding that Isis be punished for her trickery.

Ra, still reluctant to make a final judgment, agreed to move the tribunal to an island in the middle of the Nile. He instructed the ferryman Nemty not to transport any woman who looked like Isis to the island. The gods would deliberate without her interference.

Isis disguised herself as an old woman and bribed the ferryman with a gold ring. Ra was so angry when he discovered this that he punished Nemty by cutting off his toes, which is why the front of a boat's prow looks cut or broken.

Finally, the gods realized that words alone wouldn't settle this. If legal arguments couldn't convince Ra, maybe physical contests could. Let Horus and Set compete directly. Winner takes the throne. At least then there'd be a clear result instead of this endless talking.

Set agreed immediately. He was confident in his strength.

Horus agreed too. He was younger, quicker, and had the righteous fury of someone seeking to avenge his murdered father. Let Set try to defeat him.

The contests began. They would prove to be some of the strangest competitions ever devised.

The Battles of Magic and Might: From Boat Races to Hippopotamus Transformations

The gods decided that Horus and Set should compete in a boat race. Whoever won would prove his fitness to rule.

However, there was a catch. Set proposed that they build their boats from stone. Why? Well, Set was associated with the desert and unyielding strength. He thought a stone boat would demonstrate his power and solidity. The gods agreed to the terms.

Set built his boat from a mountain peak. He carved it from solid stone, thinking weight and strength would give him victory. It looked impressive.

Horus, being cleverer, cheated. He built a wooden boat and covered it with plaster painted to look like stone. It appeared to be stone but was actually light enough to float.

The race began. The gods gathered on the shore to watch. Set launched his stone boat into the Nile.

It sank immediately.

The massive stone boat plunged straight to the bottom of the river. Set had been so focused on demonstrating his strength that he'd forgotten basic physics. Stone doesn't float. Even divine stone weighs too much. He'd built himself a boat-shaped rock.

The gods watching from shore laughed. Set, the powerful god of chaos, had defeated himself through arrogance and stupidity.

Furious and humiliated, Set refused to accept defeat. If he couldn't win the race fairly, he'd prevent Horus from winning at all. He transformed himself into a hippopotamus and dove into the water, attacking Horus's boat from below.

Horus responded by transforming into a hippopotamus as well. The two divine hippos fought beneath the Nile's surface. The water churned and frothed. The gods couldn't see clearly what was happening below, but they could see the violence—the massive bodies thrashing, jaws snapping, blood clouding the water.

Hippopotamus fights are brutal. Despite their herbivore diet, hippos are among the most dangerous animals in Africa. Their jaws can bite through crocodiles. They're territorial, aggressive, and incredibly strong. Two divine hippos fighting would be even more catastrophic.

Isis stood on shore watching her son fight the god who'd murdered his father. She couldn't just stand by. She had a harpoon, its iron forged with magical spells and designed to penetrate divine flesh. She could strike Set and give Horus the advantage he needed.

So, she hurled the harpoon into the churning water, aiming for where she thought Set was thrashing.

The harpoon struck Horus instead. He screamed in pain, a sound that carried across the water even in his hippopotamus form.

Isis was horrified. She immediately began speaking spells to undo what she'd done, to extract the harpoon and heal the wound. The magical harpoon responded to her voice. It pulled free from Horus's body, and his wound began to close.

Horus surfaced in his normal form, bleeding and enraged. His mother had wounded him during battle while he fought for his life and his throne against his father's murderer.

In his fury, Horus didn't wait for explanations. He lunged from the water and attacked Isis. He drew a blade. Some texts say a knife, others a copper axe. He struck his own mother and cut off her head.

The gods watching from shore gasped in collective horror. This was matricide. Horus had just decapitated his own mother, the goddess who'd searched all of Egypt for Osiris's body, who'd hidden Horus in the marshes to save his life, who'd championed his cause for eighty years. He'd killed her in a moment of blind rage.

The severed head hit the ground. Isis's body collapsed.

Thoth reacted instantly. Using his tremendous magical power, he retrieved Isis's head and reattached it to her body. He spoke the words of healing, the magic that reversed death itself.

But something changed in the spell. When Isis's head was restored, it wasn't human anymore. Thoth had transformed it into a cow's head, the head of Hathor, the cow-headed goddess of love and motherhood. Some texts say this was an accident, a side effect of the rushed magic. Others say Thoth did it deliberately, connecting Isis to Hathor's nurturing power, making her more than she'd been before.

This beheading episode is one of the strangest parts of the *Contendings* story. It's jarring and disturbing. The hero attacks his own mother. Many other Egyptian texts ignore this incident entirely because it contradicts Isis's role as the perfect, devoted mother-goddess. The story exists in the *Contendings*, but that doesn't mean it was part of mainstream Egyptian belief. It's a variant that shows the messy, imperfect nature of this particular conflict.

Either way, Isis lived. However, Horus had still committed the act.

Ra and the assembled gods were deeply troubled. Was this really the wise, just king they wanted ruling Egypt? Or was he as violent and impulsive as Set, just with better legal claims?

The gods punished Horus. They sent him fleeing into the desert. Some texts say Ra himself went after Horus to punish him. Set was sent to capture Horus and bring him back for judgment.

Set found Horus hiding in an oasis or cave. And Set, seeing an opportunity to permanently disable his rival, attacked Horus's eyes. He tore them out, gouging them from Horus's face. Then Set took the eyes and buried them in the desert, where they transformed into lotus flowers that bloomed from the sand.

A blind god couldn't be king. A blind god couldn't maintain Ma'at or defend Egypt. Set had struck a devastating blow.

But Set made a mistake. He returned to the tribunal and lied about what happened. He told the gods he hadn't found Horus and that he must be hiding somewhere far away.

Hathor, who was either Isis in her new form or a separate goddess, went searching. She found Horus blind and suffering in the desert. To help him, she caught a gazelle and used its milk. Milk had healing properties in Egyptian medicine. She applied it to Horus's wounded eye sockets.

Slowly and miraculously, Horus's eyes regenerated. His sight returned. The injury that should have ended his claim to the throne had been healed through divine intervention.

The Eye of Horus became more than just a restored body part. It became a symbol. The wedjat eye, the stylized eye with markings beneath it, appeared everywhere in Egyptian art. People wore it as amulets for protection and healing. It was painted on boats and carved on tomb walls.

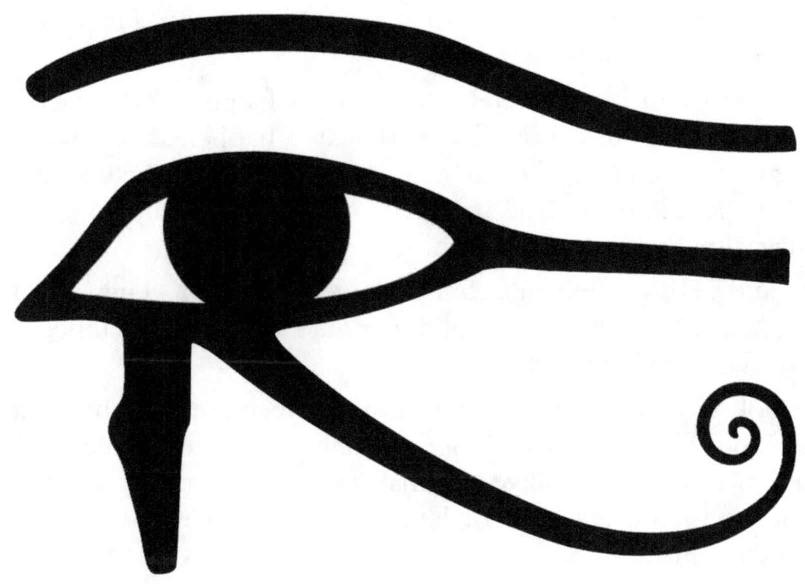

The wedjat eye.[7]

The eye represented wholeness restored. It was everything the Egyptians valued about Ma'at—balance, restoration, and the proper functioning of things that had been broken.

Mathematically, the Eye of Horus had another layer of meaning, or so later interpretations suggest. Ancient Egyptian scribes used unit fractions in all their calculations, and each part of the Eye of Horus has been linked to one: $1/2$, $1/4$, $1/8$, and so on, down to $1/64$. Add them all up, and you get $63/64$. The missing piece—the last $1/64$—was said to be the part restored by Thoth's magic when he healed Horus. It's a perfect symbol of the Egyptian worldview: logic and myth, calculation and mystery, all working together to make something whole.

With his eyes restored and transformed into a symbol of divine healing, Horus returned to the tribunal, ready to continue the fight.

What follows comes directly from *The Contendings of Horus and Set*. This episode is symbolic and mythic rather than reflecting universal Egyptian beliefs about sexuality. Set's plan was to sexually dominate Horus. In Egyptian thinking about power and status, the penetrative partner in a sexual act held dominance over the receptive partner. If Set could penetrate Horus, he'd establish his superiority. Horus would be shamed as weak and submissive.

The text says Set invited Horus to spend the night at his house. Horus agreed, perhaps not understanding Set's intention. That night, Set attempted to rape Horus.

But Horus had caught Set's semen in his hands. The next morning, Horus went to Isis and showed her what had happened. Isis was furious and disgusted. She cut off Horus's hands, the hands that held Set's semen, and threw them into the Nile so they wouldn't pollute her son. Then she used magic to grow Horus new hands.

Isis and Horus weren't finished yet, though. They devised a counterplan. If Set believed sexual dominance proved one's fitness to rule, they'd turn that logic against him.

Isis took Horus to Set's garden, where lettuce grew. Lettuce was Set's favorite food. He ate it daily. The Egyptians associated lettuce with male sexuality because the milky sap that dripped from cut lettuce stalks resembled semen. Set's love of lettuce was connected to his aggressive masculine identity.

Horus masturbated, and Isis collected his semen. She spread it on the lettuce plants in Set's garden, working it into the leaves.

The next day, Set came to his garden as usual and ate the lettuce. He consumed Horus's semen without knowing it. According to Egyptian logic, Horus had now penetrated Set, not through the usual means but through Set's mouth. Set had been made submissive, showing he was unfit to rule.

Time passed, and the tribunal reconvened. Set boasted about his sexual conquest of Horus in front of all the assembled gods. He'd dominated the younger god physically. This proved his superiority. Horus should surrender his claim.

Horus challenged this. He proposed a test. Let the gods summon Set's semen and ask where it went. If Set had truly dominated Horus, his semen would answer from inside Horus's body.

The gods agreed. They performed the magical summoning. They called to Set's semen and commanded it to identify its location.

A voice answered from the Nile, from the deep water where Isis had thrown Horus's severed hands. Set's semen was in the river, not in Horus's body. Set's claimed conquest was a lie.

Then Horus called for his own semen to reveal itself. The gods summoned it, asking where Horus's seed had gone.

A voice answered from inside Set's body. Set had been penetrated and dominated.

The gods were shocked, and many burst out laughing. Set the powerful had been completely humiliated. His attempt to prove dominance had backfired spectacularly.

Some texts say a golden disk emerged from Set's forehead at this moment, a physical manifestation of Horus's power leaving Set's body. Horus seized this disk and placed it on his own head as a crown, symbolizing that he'd taken Set's strength for himself.

The contests had proven something important. Horus was clever, determined, and capable of matching Set's strength with strategy. He might be younger, but he wasn't weak. He'd proven he could rule.

The gods were leaning decisively toward Horus. Justice, cleverness, and divine right all supported him.

The Final Verdict

At this point, Osiris himself intervened.

In some versions of the story, Osiris intervened from the underworld. From his throne in the Duat, where he ruled the dead, Osiris sent word supporting his son's claim. The texts don't all agree on the details. Some say messengers carried his words. Others suggest his will was made known through dreams or omens. However, the message was clear. Horus, as Osiris's son and heir, deserved the throne. The gods should stop delaying and restore proper order.

Osiris's support for Horus helped tip the balance. Whether through his direct intervention or simply the weight of the prolonged dispute, Ra finally made his decision.

Ra announced his verdict. Horus would be king of Egypt. He was Osiris's son and legitimate heir. The throne belonged to him by right of birth and by law. Ma'at demanded this outcome.

Set would not be executed or severely punished for his crimes. The gods needed him too much, and his power served important functions. But he would lose the throne. His reign was over.

As compensation, Set would continue in his role on the solar boat, now with greater honors. He would remain permanently stationed at the prow as the chief defender against Apep. Every night when Ra's boat traveled through the underworld, Set would stand guard with his spear, fighting the chaos serpent and protecting the sun from destruction. His voice would boom in the sky as thunder and storms, Set's power made manifest in the weather.

Set also received the two foreign goddesses, Anat and Astarte, as wives, thereby increasing his household and prestige. These Syrian warrior goddesses were fierce and powerful, making them appropriate companions for the god of strength and chaos.

Set accepted this judgment. He'd lost the throne but gained an essential role defending creation itself. His strength, his violence, his power over chaos—all of it would serve Ma'at now instead of threatening it.

Horus took the throne of Egypt. From this moment forward, every pharaoh who ruled Egypt claimed to be the "Living Horus." When a king sat on the throne, he wasn't just a human administrator. He was Horus incarnate, the divine avenger who'd reclaimed his father's throne and the legitimate ruler chosen by the gods themselves.

When a pharaoh died, he became Osiris, joining his divine father in the underworld. The new pharaoh then became Horus, continuing the cycle.

The conflict between Horus and Set wasn't just a story about two gods fighting over power. It was the foundational myth explaining legitimate kingship in Egypt. And it did so through a story that was dramatic, violent, strange, sexual, magical, and completely unforgettable.

Chapter 4: The Pantheon

Ra: The Sun God and Supreme Creator

Ra was the divine power of the sun. He was not just a god associated with the sun or a deity who controlled it from afar. Ra was the sun's consciousness, its living force. The Egyptians distinguished between the Aten, the physical solar disk, and Ra, the divine being who inhabited and animated it. When you saw the sun blazing across the sky, you were seeing Ra's body, his physical form, the source of light and life that made existence possible.

Every morning, Ra was reborn. Every evening, he descended into the underworld. Every night, he traveled through the realm of the dead. Every dawn, he emerged renewed. This daily cycle represented transformation and renewal rather than death in the human sense.

Ra appeared in Egyptian religion very early, but his importance grew over time. During the Old Kingdom (roughly 2686–2181 BCE), when the pyramids were built, Ra became the supreme god. The pharaohs declared themselves "Sons of Ra." The massive pyramid complexes at Giza incorporated solar symbolism and were designed to help the dead king join Ra in his eternal journey across the sky. Later, during the Fifth Dynasty, pharaohs built separate temples specifically dedicated to Ra. These structures were distinct from pyramid tombs, but they served similar purposes of connecting the king to the power of the sun.

The name "Ra" might come from a word meaning "sun" or "creative power," though ancient Egyptian does not always make such connections clear.

Artists depicted Ra in several forms depending on which part of his journey they wanted to emphasize. Most commonly, he appeared as a man with a falcon's head, topped with a sun disk encircled by a cobra. The cobra was the uraeus, a symbol of divine authority and protection. Ra's falcon head connected him to Horus and to the sky itself. Falcons fly high, hunt with perfect vision, and embody royal power.

Ra also appeared as a scarab beetle at dawn. The scarab was Khepri, representing the sunrise and renewal. Scarabs roll balls of dung across the ground to lay their eggs, and the Egyptians saw this as a perfect image for the sun being pushed across the sky. Khepri meant "he who comes into being." He was the creative force of each new day.

At sunset, Ra became Atum, the ancient creator god from the Ennead. Atum was the evening sun, the aged god descending into the underworld. These three aspects—Khepri, Ra, and Atum— were the sun's daily cycle from birth through strength to death and rebirth.

Ra's daily journey was both glorious and dangerous. During the day, he sailed across the sky in a boat called the Mandjet, the "Boat of Millions of Years." The sky was not empty space; it was water, an extension of the cosmic ocean Nu that

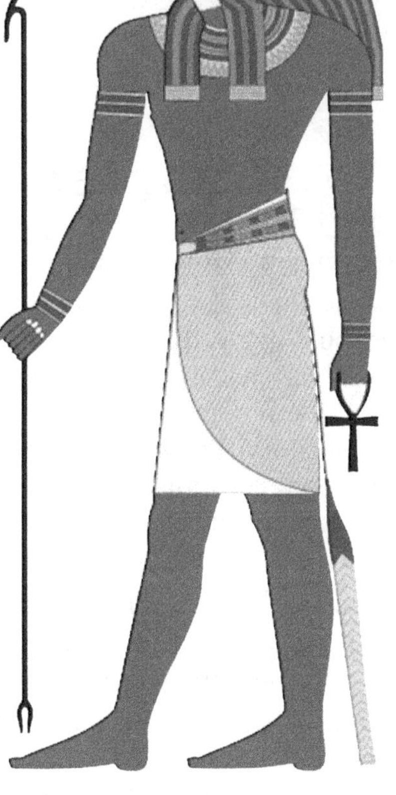

A depiction of Ra.'

had existed before creation. Ra sailed on this celestial Nile, traveling from east to west, bringing light to the world below.

His boat carried divine passengers, though the gods who accompanied Ra varied depending on the text and time period. Ma'at, the goddess of truth and order, often sailed with him to keep cosmic balance. Thoth sometimes appeared as a navigator. Abstract concepts like Sia (divine perception) and Hu (authoritative speech) might be personified as crew members in texts like the *Book of Gates* and the *Amduat.* To put it simply, Ra did not travel alone. He traveled with the forces necessary to maintain Ma'at and protect creation.

At sunset, Ra's boat entered the underworld, the Duat, through the western horizon. Here began the most dangerous part of the journey. The underworld was not just the realm of the dead. It was the place where chaos threatened to break through, where the ordered world could unravel, and where the sun could be destroyed and morning would never come.

The biggest threat was Apep.

Apep (also called Apophis) was a gigantic serpent of chaos. He was not a god. Apep was an anti-god, anti-creation, and anti-existence. He embodied the chaos that existed before the universe and still lurked at its edges, trying to return everything to primordial nothingness. Every night, Apep tried to swallow Ra's boat. If he succeeded, the sun would not rise. The world would end.

Set often appears in texts about Ra, standing at the prow with his spear, fighting the chaos serpent every single night. This was Set's great purpose after losing the throne. Other texts describe Mehen, a giant protective serpent who coiled around Ra's cabin to shield him from danger. Either way, Ra needed defending. The defender would spear or repel Apep repeatedly, but Apep could never be killed permanently. He was chaos. You cannot destroy chaos, only contain it. Every night, the battle repeated.

Sometimes Apep partially succeeded. When the sun dimmed or disappeared, during eclipses, storms, or unusual periods of darkness, the Egyptians knew Apep had gained a temporary advantage. Priests performed rituals to help Ra escape and drive Apep back. They recited spells, made offerings, and created wax figures of Apep that they burned or stabbed to magically harm the serpent. The rituals worked because the sun always returned. Ra always won, and Ma'at always prevailed.

After defeating Apep, Ra continued through the twelve hours of the night, passing through twelve regions of the Duat. Each hour had its own dangers, challenges, and divine beings. Ra encountered the blessed dead who lived in the underworld, including Osiris himself. Some texts describe conversations between Ra and Osiris, the sun of the living meeting the king of the dead, both maintaining different aspects of creation.

At dawn, Ra emerged reborn from the eastern horizon. The Egyptians saw the sunrise as a birth, Ra literally being born from the sky goddess Nut. Every morning was creation happening again. Every dawn proved that Ma'at still functioned, that chaos had not won, and that life would continue.

Ra's supremacy was not unchallenged. During the Middle Kingdom (roughly 2055–1650 BCE), another god named Amun rose to prominence in the city of Thebes. Amun was "the Hidden One," the god of air and creative power. As Thebes became politically powerful, so did its patron god. Eventually, priests combined Amun with Ra, creating Amun-Ra, a god who was both the invisible force of creation and the visible sun.

This didn't confuse the ancient Egyptians. They were fine with gods being complicated. Amun-Ra could be one god with two faces, two gods working together, or the same power showing up in different forms. The ancient texts don't always explain which one because the writers didn't think they needed to. A god could be all of these things at once, and that was just how it worked.

Ra also merged with Atum, becoming Ra-Atum, and with Khepri as Ra-Khepri. Gods blended, separated, and recombined depending on which attributes people wanted to emphasize. This flexibility allowed the Egyptian religion to adapt and evolve over three thousand years while maintaining continuity.

Ra remained important in Egyptian religion throughout its history. Every pharaoh was considered his son. Every day proved his power. Every sunrise was a miracle, not because the Egyptians were primitive and did not understand astronomy but because they understood that existence itself was miraculous.

When someone died and traveled through the Duat, they joined Ra's journey. The blessed dead sailed with Ra in his boat, defending against Apep.

However, Ra was not always gentle or kind. He was the sun, blazing, harsh, and sometimes deadly. Too much sun killed crops, caused drought, and burned skin. Ra's power was necessary, but it was also dangerous. The Egyptians respected him the way you respect fire; it was essential for life but capable of great destruction.

Later foreign rulers of Egypt, such as the Greeks and Romans, identified Ra with their own sun gods, particularly Helios and Apollo. But Ra was distinctly Egyptian. He was not just a god who drove a sun chariot or represented solar power. He was creation itself, maintaining existence through his daily journey and proving every dawn that Ma'at still functioned and chaos had not won.

Thoth: The God of Wisdom, Writing, and Magic

If Ra was power and authority, Thoth was knowledge and cleverness. If Ra represented the obvious might of the sun, Thoth represented the subtle power of words, mathematics, and magic. Ra helped create the physical world. Thoth gave it meaning by inventing the words to describe it.

Thoth's most important role was as the inventor of writing. The Egyptians credited Thoth with creating hieroglyphs, the sacred script that preserved knowledge, recorded history, and made civilization possible. Writing was not just a practical tool. It was divine magic. Words had power. The right words, written correctly, could heal, protect, curse, or compel. And Thoth knew all the words.

Artists depicted Thoth in two main forms: as a man with an ibis head or as a baboon. The ibis was a wading bird with a long, curved beak. It is commonly found along the Nile. Ibises were associated with wisdom because they seemed methodical and careful, probing the mud for food with precision. The ibis's curved beak also resembled the crescent moon, connecting Thoth to lunar cycles.

As a baboon, Thoth appeared squatting or standing, often holding the Eye of Horus or a writing palette. Baboons chattered at dawn, seeming to greet the sunrise, which made them sacred to both Ra and Thoth. The baboon form emphasized Thoth's role as scribe and record keeper, as baboons have dexterous hands suitable for writing.

Thoth's name might derive from "Djehuty," which could mean "he who is like the ibis," though the etymology is uncertain. What is certain is his portfolio. He was the god of writing, knowledge, science, magic, arbitration, truth, and timekeeping. He was the moon god, measuring time by the

Thoth.[9]

moon's phases. He was also Ra's secretary, recording the gods' decisions and maintaining divine archives.

In creation myths, Thoth often appears as a problem-solver. Remember when Set murdered Osiris and scattered his body? Anubis and Isis reassembled Osiris, but Thoth provided the spells to restore him. When Horus lost his eye fighting Set, Thoth (or Hathor, depending on the version) healed it. When the tribunal could not decide between Horus and Set, Thoth advocated for justice and proper procedure. Thoth was the god you called when things went wrong and clever thinking could fix them.

Thoth was also the god of magic, or *heka* in Egyptian. Magic and knowledge were connected. Knowing something's true name gave you power over it. Knowing the right spells lets you command reality. Thoth knew more true names and more spells than anyone except possibly Isis. His magic was intellectual, based on understanding rather than raw power.

Many magical texts began with invocations to Thoth. Spells for protection, healing, or transformation called on Thoth's authority. Doctors (who were also priests and magicians) considered themselves Thoth's servants. Scribes made offerings to Thoth before beginning important work. Anyone who worked with words, numbers, or knowledge honored Thoth.

In the judgment of the dead, Thoth played a crucial role. When someone died and traveled through the Duat, they eventually reached the Hall of Two Truths, where Osiris sat in judgment. The heart of the deceased was placed on a scale opposite the feather of Ma'at. If the heart was lighter than the feather, meaning the person had lived according to Ma'at, they could proceed to the afterlife. If heavier, meaning they were corrupted by sin, the heart was fed to Ammit the Devourer, and the person ceased to exist.

Thoth supervised this weighing. He stood beside the scales with his writing palette and recorded the result. His honesty was absolute. He would not falsify records to save anyone. However, he was also fair. If the scales balanced perfectly, Thoth spoke on the deceased's behalf to Osiris, explaining that this person deserved eternal life.

One of the most important Egyptian texts is the *Book of Thoth*, though ironically, no complete copy exists. References to it appear in other texts, describing it as containing Thoth's most powerful magic. It had spells for understanding the language of animals, for commanding nature, and for seeing the gods themselves. Magicians claimed to have fragments of the *Book of Thoth,* so finding the complete book became a legendary quest in Egyptian magical lore.

Later, during the Greco-Roman period, Greeks associated Thoth with their god Hermes, creating Hermes Trismegistus ("Thrice-Great Hermes"). This syncretized figure became central to Hermetic philosophy and alchemy. The Greeks saw Thoth's wisdom and Hermes's role as messenger and trickster as compatible. Hermes Trismegistus allegedly wrote the Emerald Tablet and other mystical texts that influenced medieval and Renaissance magic.

But the original Egyptian Thoth was not a trickster who caused mischief. He was a responsible administrator, a wise counselor, and a keeper of records. He solved problems through knowledge rather than chaos. He represented everything civilization needed to function: written laws, mathematical precision, astronomical calendars, medical knowledge, and fair arbitration of disputes.

Priests and scribes were Thoth's primary worshipers. His main cult center was Hermopolis (called Khemenu in Egyptian), where he was honored alongside the Ogdoad. Scribes would pour a libation of water, a few drops from their water jar, onto the ground before beginning to write, dedicating their work to Thoth.

Thoth had a female counterpart, Seshat, the goddess of writing, architecture, mathematics, and record-keeping. She appeared as a woman wearing a leopard-skin dress (the mark of the priesthood) with a seven-pointed star or flower symbol above her head. The symbol might have represented a stylized hemp plant or simply been a unique identifier.

While Thoth invented writing and possessed all knowledge, Seshat specialized in applying that knowledge practically. She was the goddess of libraries and archives, keeping records for all eternity. She measured and recorded the years of pharaohs' reigns, recording how long each king ruled and what he accomplished.

Seshat also played a crucial role in temple construction through the "stretching of the cord" ceremony. Before building a temple, the pharaoh and Seshat performed a ritual in which they used surveying cords to measure and align the building with the stars. Seshat ensured the temple's proportions were correct, its orientation was astronomically precise, and its measurements followed sacred geometry. Every major temple in Egypt was thought to be aligned and measured under Seshat's guidance.

She appeared in royal inscriptions recording military victories, tribute collected, and foreign captives taken. When pharaohs boasted about their conquests on temple walls, Seshat was shown recording the numbers, tallying prisoners, counting gold, and measuring captured land. Her records made the pharaoh's achievements permanent and official.

Though less famous than Thoth, Seshat was essential to scribes, architects, and anyone who worked with measurements or permanent records. Thoth provided the knowledge; Seshat made sure it was recorded accurately and used correctly. Together, they represented the intellectual foundations of Egyptian civilization.

Thoth mattered because knowledge mattered. The Egyptians built one of history's great civilizations through organization, record-keeping, and accumulated wisdom. Thoth and Seshat represented all of that. Without them, there would be no written language, no mathematics, no magic, no fair judgment of the dead, and no way to preserve knowledge across generations. Ra might have provided the power of creation, but Thoth and Seshat provided the knowledge to use that creation wisely.

Anubis: Guardian of the Dead and Master of Mummification

Anubis walked the boundary between life and death. He was the jackal-headed god who guided souls through the underworld, who invented mummification, who protected the dead from harm, and who stood beside Osiris during the judgment of souls.

His appearance was striking and immediately recognizable. He had a man's body with the head of a black jackal (or sometimes a wild dog). The black color was not natural animal coloring; it was symbolic. Black represented the fertile soil of Egypt, the regenerative power of the Nile's flood, and the preservation of mummified bodies, which turned black from the resins used in mummification.

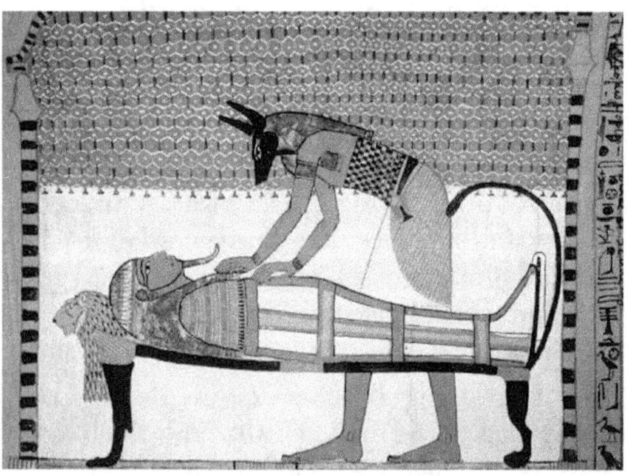

Anubis attending a mummy.[10]

Why a jackal? Jackals scavenged in cemeteries, digging up improperly buried bodies. This made them threats to the dead. The Egyptians turned this threat into a protector. Make the jackal god the guardian of graves, and real jackals might leave burials alone. It was the same principle that made Set the defender against Apep. The Egyptians were redirecting dangerous forces toward protecting what they once threatened.

Anubis's most famous role was in mummification. According to myth, he performed the first mummification when he prepared Osiris's body after Set murdered and dismembered him. Working with Isis, Anubis washed Osiris's reassembled body, removed his organs, dried the flesh with natron, wrapped it in linen, and performed the Opening of the Mouth ceremony to restore the senses. Historically, mummification techniques evolved over centuries during the Early Dynastic Period, but Egyptians saw Anubis' process as the prototype.

Every embalming that followed was a reenactment of what Anubis did for Osiris. Embalmers were called "priests of Anubis" and wore jackal masks while performing the rituals. When they wrapped the body in linen, they were Anubis wrapping Osiris.

The mummification process took seventy days total: forty days for the body to dry completely in natron and thirty days for wrapping and final preparations. During this time, the deceased's family maintained vigil, made offerings, and recited prayers. Anubis oversaw every step, ensuring the process was done correctly.

But Anubis's role did not end when mummification finished. He guided the soul through the Duat. After death, the soul, specifically the *ba*, which will be discussed more in Chapter 5, had to navigate a dangerous journey through the underworld. The Duat had demons, monsters, and magical challenges. Without guidance, a soul could be lost, trapped, or destroyed.

Anubis led them through the twelve gates, past the guardians, and to the Hall of Two Truths, where Osiris judged them. This guidance was so important that funeral prayers frequently invoked Anubis by name: "May Anubis protect you. May he guide your steps in the darkness. May he speak on your behalf before Osiris."

In the Hall of Two Truths, Anubis supervised the weighing of the heart. He operated the scales, ensuring perfect balance. When Thoth recorded the results, Anubis confirmed the accuracy. If the heart weighed the same as Ma'at's feather, Anubis led the deceased to Osiris and declared them worthy of eternal life.

If the heart was heavy with sin, Anubis stepped aside. Ammit the Devourer, a monster with a crocodile's head, a lion's forequarters, and a hippopotamus's back end, devoured the heavy heart. The person ceased to exist entirely. This was the second death, the final death. It meant complete annihilation.

Anubis's honesty was absolute. He could not be bribed, tricked, or swayed by emotion. The scales were the scales, and the heart weighed what it weighed. Ma'at demanded truth, and Anubis enforced that demand without mercy or favoritism. Rich or poor, pharaoh or farmer, priest or criminal, Anubis treated everyone the same in death.

His major cult center was Cynopolis (called Hardai in Egyptian), meaning "City of Dogs." Here, jackals were sacred and protected. People brought mummified jackal cubs as offerings, dedicating them to Anubis. The city's priests were experts in mummification and funerary rites.

Anubis had complicated relationships with other death gods. Sometimes he was Osiris's son. Different myths give different mothers, including Nephthys or the goddess Bast. Other times, he appeared as a separate deity who simply served Osiris. The texts do not always clarify because the exact genealogy mattered less than his function. Anubis served the dead, worked for Osiris, and maintained the proper operations of the afterlife.

Before Osiris became the dominant god of death during the Old Kingdom, Anubis might have been the supreme ruler of the dead. As Osiris's cult grew, Anubis's role shifted from ruler to servant, from king of the dead to guardian and guide. But this shift did not diminish his importance. Every dead person still needed Anubis. Every mummy still required his blessing. Every journey through the Duat still needed his guidance.

Prayers to Anubis filled tombs throughout Egypt. "Anubis, foremost of the western gods, master of the sacred land, he who is upon his mountain..." The "western gods" meant the gods of the dead since the west was where the sun set and souls entered the underworld. The "sacred land" was the necropolis, the cemetery. The "mountain" referred to the desert cliffs where tombs were carved.

Anubis appeared on coffins, tomb walls, canopic jars that held mummified organs, amulets, and funerary masks. His image meant protection. It meant the proper rituals had been performed and that the deceased had a powerful ally in the dangerous afterlife.

One important detail to mention: Anubis was not scary or evil despite his association with death. He was protective, professional, and necessary. Death was not a horror to the Egyptians; it was a transition. And Anubis made that transition possible. He was like a skilled guide leading you through treacherous mountains at night. You would be grateful for his expertise rather than frightened by his presence.

The Greeks later associated Anubis with their own supernatural guide, Hermes, though they kept Anubis distinct enough to remain recognizable. In Greco-Roman Egypt, Anubis was still popular and important. People continued invoking him for protection in death long after Egypt's political power faded.

For anyone planning to die in ancient Egypt, which was everyone, Anubis was essential. You wanted your body to be mummified correctly. You wanted to navigate the Duat successfully. You wanted your heart to balance in judgment. You wanted eternal life. Anubis made all of that possible. Without him, death was just death. It would be final, terrifying, and meaningless. With him, death was a doorway to eternity.

Bastet, Sekhmet, and Hathor: The Fierce and Gentle Goddesses

Three major goddesses—Bastet, Sekhmet, and Hathor—shared complex relationships, overlapping roles, and sometimes merged identities. Understanding them means understanding how Egyptian gods could be distinct and connected at the same time, as well as how a goddess could be both a protective mother and a bloodthirsty destroyer.

Let's start with Bastet, the cat goddess.

Bastet appeared as a woman with a cat's head or sometimes as a full cat. In earlier periods, she looked more lionlike and fierce. Later, especially during the Late Period, after 664 BCE, she became gentler and more associated with domestic cats than wild lions.

Cats were sacred in Egypt for obvious reasons. Cats killed snakes and rats, protecting grain stores and homes from vermin. In a civilization that depended on grain harvests, cats were essential. They were also elegant, independent, and mysterious, qualities the Egyptians admired.

Bastet.[11]

Bastet's main cult center was Bubastis in the Nile Delta. Her temple there was magnificent, described by the Greek historian Herodotus as one of Egypt's most beautiful structures, surrounded by water like an island. Annual festivals at Bubastis drew massive crowds. Some accounts claim 700,000 people attended, though that number is probably exaggerated. The festivals involved music, dancing, drinking, and celebrating fertility and joy.

People brought mummified cats as offerings to Bastet. Archaeologists have found massive cat cemeteries near her temples. There were hundreds of thousands of mummified cats, many of them kittens, carefully wrapped and buried. Some were beloved pets. Others were specifically raised and ritually killed as offerings. This seems brutal to modern sensibilities, but the Egyptians saw it as honoring Bastet by sending her servants in the form of sacred animals.

Bastet represented home, fertility, joy, music, dancing, and protection. She was the goddess of domestic life, of women and children, and of the pleasures of civilization. She protected homes from evil spirits and disease. She brought happiness and abundance. She was one of the most beloved and accessible goddesses, not distant or terrifying but present in everyday life.

But Bastet had a fiercer aspect. Sometimes she appeared as a lioness, blurring the line between her and Sekhmet. This brings us to the next goddess.

Sekhmet was Bastet's terrifying sister or alternate form. She appeared as a woman with a lioness's head, usually wearing red, the color of blood, and carrying weapons. Her name meant "She Who Is Powerful" or "the Powerful One." Everything about Sekhmet screamed danger.

Sekhmet was war, plague, destruction, and divine fury. When Ra sent his Eye to punish rebellious humanity, it became Sekhmet. She slaughtered humans by the thousands, wading through blood, drunk on violence. Only Ra's trick with beer dyed to look like

A relief of Sekhmet.[12]

blood stopped her rampage. When she finally calmed down, she transformed from Sekhmet into Hathor, whom we will discuss next.

This transformation is key. Sekhmet and Hathor were not separate beings. They were the same goddess in different aspects. The Eye of Ra, the fierce daughter who enacted her father's will, could be Sekhmet the destroyer or Hathor the gentle.

Priests of Sekhmet were doctors. This makes sense. The goddess who brought plague could also cure it. The power that destroyed could also heal. Sekhmet's priests were experts in medicine, magic, and the healing arts. They invoked Sekhmet to both cause and prevent disease, understanding that she controlled both sides of that equation.

Her main temple was in Memphis. People made offerings to Sekhmet, asking for protection from disease, healing from illness, success in battle, or vengeance against enemies. She was dangerous, but her danger could be directed. Appeal to her correctly, and she would destroy your problems instead of you.

One peculiar detail is that hundreds of statues of Sekhmet were erected by Pharaoh Amenhotep III, possibly as many as 730, two for every day of the year. These statues stood in his mortuary temple at Thebes. Scholars debate why there were so many, perhaps to honor every possible aspect of Sekhmet, to contain and appease her destructive power, or simply because Amenhotep III wanted overwhelming divine protection in the afterlife.

Now, let us talk about Hathor. She appeared as a woman with cow's horns and a sun disk between them or sometimes as a full cow. Cows were sacred to the ancient Egyptians. Cows gave milk, sustaining life. They were gentle, nurturing mothers. Hathor embodied these qualities.

Her name meant "House of Horus," meaning she sheltered Horus, the king. She was a mother goddess, associated with queens and divine motherhood that supported kingship. When pharaohs claimed to be the Living Horus, their mothers or wives were associated with Hathor.

Hathor's roles were extensive. She was the goddess of love, beauty, music, dance, joy, motherhood, fertility, drunkenness, and foreign lands. She was a patron of miners because important mines were in foreign deserts, of dancers and musicians, of lovers, of women giving birth, and of anyone seeking joy and abundance.

Her main temple was at Dendera, and it is one of the best preserved temple complexes in Egypt. The temple's ceiling showed astronomical scenes with Hathor as a cow carrying the sun. Festivals at Dendera celebrated Hathor with music, dancing, and ritual drunkenness. Yes, getting drunk was part of worshiping Hathor. Remember how Ra stopped Sekhmet's rampage by making her drunk? Alcohol transformed Sekhmet into Hathor, so drunkenness became sacred to her.

Hathor's temple at Denedra.[18]

Hathor also had a death aspect. She was "Lady of the West," goddess of the necropolis. She greeted the dead as they entered the afterlife, offering them refreshment and comfort.

But here is where it gets complex. Bastet, Sekhmet, and Hathor were not always distinct. They could merge, separate, or be aspects of each other depending on the context and time period. They were genuinely distinct goddesses with their own cults, temples, and identities. But they could also take on the role of the Eye of Ra, the fierce power that Ra sent forth to accomplish his will. When functioning as the Eye of Ra, Sekhmet brought destruction, Bastet brought protection, and Hathor brought nurturing power. The Egyptians did not see this as confusing. Multiple goddesses could embody the same divine function when needed.

During different periods, the emphasis shifted. In the Old Kingdom, Hathor was more prominent. In the New Kingdom, Sekhmet gained importance. During the Late Period, Bastet's gentler cat form became extremely popular. However, they still remained connected.

One myth ties them together beautifully. The Eye of Ra became angry and fled to Nubia, south of Egypt. Ra sent Thoth and Shu to bring her back. They found her as a fierce lioness, Sekhmet. Through clever words and promises, they convinced her to return to Egypt. As she traveled north, she gradually calmed down, transforming from a lioness into a domestic cat, Bastet, and finally arriving in Egypt as the gentle cow goddess Hathor. The journey from south to north (the way the Nile flows) paralleled her transformation from fierce to gentle.

This myth explains seasonal changes, the Nile's flood, and the nature of divine power. It could be destructive or nurturing, but it was always the same core energy.

Women especially honored these goddesses. Pregnant women invoked Hathor's protection. Women called on Bastet to protect their children. Healing from illness might require appeasing Sekhmet. Defending your home meant invoking Bastet. These goddesses were present in women's daily lives in ways male gods often were not.

The Greeks later identified Hathor with Aphrodite, the goddess of love and beauty, and Bastet with Artemis, the goddess of hunting and wilderness. But the Egyptian versions were distinct. They were not just deities of love, war, or hunting. They could be fierce and gentle, destructive and creative, all at once.

Bes and Taweret: Protectors of Home and Childbirth

Not all Egyptian gods were majestic and beautiful. Some were deliberately grotesque, strange-looking, and more comical than dignified. Bes and Taweret fell into this category. They were household gods who protected ordinary people from everyday dangers, especially during childbirth.

Bes looked like no other Egyptian god. He was a dwarf with a lion's mane. He had a bearded face that made a fierce or comical expression (it was hard to tell which), and was bow-legged, with his tongue sometimes sticking out. He wore a feathered headdress and might carry knives or musical instruments. He looked more like a gargoyle than a god.

An amulet depicting Bes.[14]

His appearance was deliberately scary. Bes frightened away demons and evil spirits through his sheer grotesqueness. Demons were used to dealing with dignified, beautiful gods. Bes caught them off guard. His bizarre appearance, loud music, and threatening postures drove away anything malicious.

Bes was not actually a single god. "Bes" was more like a category covering several similar dwarf deities. Over time, they merged into one figure that Egyptians simply called Bes. His origins were probably foreign, maybe from Nubia or Punt, but he became thoroughly Egyptian.

Bes protected homes, especially sleeping areas and places where children were born. His image appeared on beds, headrests, mirrors, cosmetic containers, and bedroom walls. Homes needed protection from demons, snakes, scorpions, and nightmares. Bes provided that protection through his fierce appearance and his role as a guardian.

He was especially important during childbirth. Birth was dangerous in the ancient world. Maternal mortality was high, infant mortality was higher, and complications could kill both mother and child. Evil spirits were thought to threaten newborns and mothers during this vulnerable time.

Bes stood guard during birth. His image was carved into birthing bricks, special bricks on which women squatted while giving birth. His face stared out, threatening any demon that approached. Women in labor called on Bes for protection. Midwives invoked his name. After birth, amulets of Bes were placed near the baby to keep it safe.

Bes also represented joy, music, and sexuality. He played musical instruments, drums, harps, and tambourines. He also danced. Music and laughter drove away evil, so Bes was associated with festive occasions, drinking, and celebration. He appeared on wine jars and at feasts. Brothels and taverns displayed his image.

Despite his importance to ordinary Egyptians, Bes did not have major temples. He did not have an elaborate priesthood or mythology. He was a folk god, popular with common people who needed everyday protection more than cosmic drama. Rich and poor alike displayed his image in their homes.

Now let us talk about Taweret.

Taweret looked even stranger than Bes. She had a hippopotamus head, a crocodile tail, lion's paws, pendulous human breasts, and a pregnant belly. She stood upright on her hind legs, sometimes carrying a knife or the protective *sa* symbol, a hieroglyph that represented protection. She looked monstrous, and that was the point.

A statuette of Taweret.[15]

Like Bes, Taweret's fearsome appearance scared away evil. But while Bes generally protected everyone, Taweret specialized in protecting pregnant women and mothers.

Her name meant "the Great One" or "the Great Female." Hippopotamuses were dangerous, highly territorial, aggressive, and protective of their young. A mother hippo was one of the most dangerous animals in Africa. Taweret channeled that protective maternal ferocity toward guarding human mothers.

Pregnant women wore Taweret amulets for protection. Images of Taweret decorated bedrooms and birthing areas. Midwives invoked her name. She protected both mother and child from demons, miscarriage, complications, and postpartum dangers.

Taweret also appeared in connection with the afterlife. Some texts describe her standing near the Lake of Fire in the Duat, preventing evil souls from escaping judgment.

Like Bes, Taweret did not have major temples or a complex mythology. She was a practical goddess for practical problems. However, her popularity was immense. Every mother needed protection during birth. Everyone knew someone who had died in childbirth or lost a baby. Taweret mattered personally in ways the great cosmic gods sometimes did not.

One interesting detail is that Taweret was associated with the northern night sky. She held back dangerous forces in the northern sky, protecting order. This minor detail shows that even simple household gods were connected to larger cosmic principles.

Both Bes and Taweret represented something important about Egyptian religion. It served real people's needs. Yes, there were cosmic dramas about Ra fighting Apep and Horus battling Set. But there were also pregnant women hoping to survive childbirth, parents trying to protect their children from disease, and families needing protection from snakes in the night.

Bes and Taweret were gods you could call on personally. They did not require priests as intermediaries. They did not demand elaborate rituals or expensive offerings. You could paint Bes's face on your bedroom wall yourself. You could wear a cheap Taweret amulet. These gods were accessible.

Sobek and Khnum: Gods of the Nile's Power and Fertility

The Nile was Egypt's life. Agriculture, trade, transportation, drinking water, fish, birds, and papyrus for writing all depended on the river. Egyptian religion reflected this reality by including several deities associated with the Nile's power, its creatures, and its annual flood. Sobek and Khnum are two major examples.

Sobek was the crocodile god. He appeared as a man with a crocodile head or sometimes as a full crocodile wearing a crown. Crocodiles were terrifying predators that killed people regularly. They lurked in the Nile and canals, attacking anyone who came too close. Making the crocodile into a god was classic Egyptian logic. Take something dangerous and make it sacred so you can negotiate with it rather than just fear it.

A statue of Sobek from the Twelfth Dynasty.[16]

Sobek represented the Nile's raw power, strength, danger, and ability to take life as well as give it. He was the god of fertility and protection, military might, and royal authority. Pharaohs associated themselves with Sobek to emphasize their own power and ferocity.

His main cult centers were in the Faiyum Oasis, an area of lakes fed by the Nile, and at Kom Ombo in southern Egypt. The temple at Kom Ombo is particularly interesting because it was a double temple dedicated to both Sobek and Horus. The temple had two parallel sections that were perfectly symmetrical, one for each god.

At Sobek's temples, priests kept sacred crocodiles. These crocodiles lived in temple pools, were fed choice meat and wine, and wore gold jewelry. When they died, they were mummified and buried with full honors. The temples also maintained crocodile breeding areas. Some estimates suggest that over two thousand mummified crocodiles have been found in Sobek's cult centers.

Why keep crocodiles in temples? Having a living crocodile present made the god more real and more immediate. The sacred crocodiles were Sobek made flesh. Feeding them was feeding the god. Honoring them was honoring the god. And if a sacred crocodile attacked someone, that was Sobek's will being enacted directly.

Sobek protected fishermen and people living near the Nile. Prayers to Sobek asked for safety from crocodiles and success in fishing. Amulets of Sobek provided protection when traveling on water. Soldiers invoked Sobek before battle, seeking his fierce strength.

Over time, Sobek merged with Ra, becoming Sobek-Ra. The crocodile god gained solar attributes, representing the sun's power to sustain life through the Nile's fertility and take life through the crocodile's attacks. This merger elevated Sobek from a regional deity to a more cosmic figure.

Now, let us talk about Khnum, a very different Nile god.

Khnum appeared as a man with a ram's head, but not just any ram. It was a specific breed with horizontal, wavy horns that curled forward. This was the ancient Egyptian ram breed, and it was different from the curved-horn rams that later became common.

A statuette of Khnum from the Late Period.[17]

Khnum was a creator god. His main role was fashioning humans on a potter's wheel. He did not create humanity as a species—that was Ra's or Atum's work—but he crafted individual people, giving each person their specific form. According to some texts, particularly later royal inscriptions, this creation included the person's *ka*, their spiritual double or life force, which will be explained more fully in Chapter 5.

Khnum's main cult center was on Elephantine Island at Aswan, near the Nile's First Cataract. This southern location placed him at what the Egyptians considered the source of the Nile. Khnum controlled the flood, releasing it from the Nile's mythical source each year.

The flood was everything to the ancient Egyptians. Too little water meant drought and famine. Too much meant destroyed villages and ruined fields. The flood needed to be exactly right. Khnum controlled this balance, making him one of Egypt's most important gods.

One famous story on the Famine Stele describes a seven-year drought during the reign of Pharaoh Djoser, though the stele itself was carved much later. The Nile did not flood properly, so crops failed, and people starved. Djoser asked his vizier, Imhotep, what to do. Imhotep researched and discovered that Khnum controlled the flood. Djoser made generous offerings to Khnum's temple on Elephantine Island. Khnum was pleased and restored the proper flood. Egypt was saved.

This story emphasized Khnum's power and the importance of honoring him. It also showed the pharaoh's role as an intermediary between the gods and the people. When things went wrong, the king had to repair the relationship with the appropriate deity.

Khnum had two consorts, depending on the location, Satis and Anuket. Satis was the goddess of hunting and the annual flood's initial rush of water. Anuket was the goddess of the Nile's cataracts and rapids. Together, Khnum, Satis, and Anuket formed a divine family governing the Nile's southern source.

Rams were sacred to Khnum. At his temples, rams were kept, honored, and, when they died, mummified. The connection between rams and fertility was obvious. Rams were virile and aggressive breeders. Khnum's ram form linked him to fertility, creation, and life-giving power.

Neither god had the cosmic importance of Ra or Osiris. However, regional power was still real power. If you lived in the Faiyum, Sobek was your primary god. If you lived near Aswan, Khnum was more important. The great cosmic myths mattered, but so did local concerns, local gods, and local needs.

Amun and Amun-Ra: The Hidden One Who Became Supreme

Amun started as a relatively minor deity and became one of Egypt's most powerful gods. His rise paralleled the political rise of Thebes, the city where he was the patron deity. By the New Kingdom (1550–1077 BCE), Amun had merged with Ra to become Amun-Ra, King of the

Gods. He was worshiped throughout Egypt and beyond.

His name meant "the Hidden One" or "the Invisible One." Amun represented the unseen creative force that permeated everything. You could not see him, but his power was everywhere. He was the breath of life, the creative energy that animated creation, and the mystery behind existence.

Artists depicted Amun as a man wearing a crown with two tall plumes. Sometimes he had blue or black skin. He could also appear as a ram, like Khnum, but with different curved horns, or as a goose. The ram form connected him to fertility and creative power. The goose form linked him to creation myths in which the cosmic egg was laid by a celestial goose.

Amun's origins were ancient. He appeared in the Ogdoad of Hermopolis as one of the eight primordial deities representing pre-creation chaos. Amun and his female counterpart, Amaunet, represented "hiddenness," the unknowable aspect of the state before creation. But as Thebes grew politically powerful during the Middle Kingdom, Amun separated from his Hermopolitan origins and became Thebes's supreme deity.

The New Kingdom changed everything. Thebes became Egypt's capital. The pharaohs of the Eighteenth Dynasty, including Ahmose, Hatshepsut, Thutmose III, and Amenhotep III, were Theban and credited Amun with their military victories and political success. Every conquest proved Amun's power. Every treasure taken in war enriched Amun's temples. The more Egypt succeeded, the more Amun's glory grew.

Amun merged with Ra, becoming Amun-Ra. This fusion created a god who was both the hidden creative principle, Amun, and the visible sun, Ra. Amun-Ra was the ultimate divine power. He was present everywhere but visible nowhere, creating everything while remaining mysterious.

Amun.[18]

The Karnak Temple complex in Thebes became Amun's main sanctuary and one of the largest religious structures ever built.

Construction continued for about two thousand years. The Hypostyle Hall alone, just one part of the complex, had 134 massive columns, some 70 feet tall. The whole complex covered over two hundred acres.

Amun's priesthood became incredibly wealthy and powerful. They controlled vast lands, employed thousands of workers, collected tribute from conquered territories, and influenced political decisions. At one point during the New Kingdom, Amun's high priest rivaled the pharaoh in wealth and authority. This caused tensions. One pharaoh, Akhenaten, actually tried to abolish Amun's worship entirely, a topic discussed later, though the attempt failed.

Amun was called "King of the Gods," which might seem to contradict Ra's supremacy. However, the Egyptians saw no contradiction. Amun-Ra was one god, two gods merged as one, or two aspects of the same divine principle. The Egyptians were comfortable with this ambiguity. They did not need neat theological categories. Gods could be multiple things at the same time.

Pharaohs claimed to be Amun's sons. Royal inscriptions described how Amun took the form of the reigning pharaoh and impregnated the queen, making the next pharaoh literally Amun's child. Hatshepsut, one of Egypt's few female pharaohs, used this divine birth story to legitimize her rule. Temple reliefs at Deir el-Bahari show Amun visiting her mother and Hatshepsut being born as Amun's daughter.

The oracle of Amun made important decisions. When difficult political or military questions arose, priests would ask Amun's statue for guidance. The statue, carried on poles by priests, would supposedly move to indicate yes or no answers. Scholars debate whether this was a genuine belief or political theater, but it does not matter. What matters is that people accepted Amun's oracle as authoritative. Gods spoke through statues, and Amun's word was final.

Foreign peoples even adopted Amun's worship. As Egypt conquered Nubia, Syria, and other territories, Amun temples appeared in those regions. Even after Egypt's power declined, Amun worship continued in Nubia for centuries. The Greeks identified Amun with Zeus, their king of the gods. Alexander the Great visited the oracle of Amun at Siwa Oasis and was proclaimed Amun's son, using this divine legitimacy to rule Egypt.

Amun represented the mysterious power behind everything. You could see Ra blazing in the sky. You could feel the Nile's water. You could watch crops growing. But what caused all of that? What was the hidden force making existence possible? Amun was the answer.

Later religions with one all-powerful god would develop similar ideas, an invisible creator distinct from the physical world. Amun embraced this concept first.

Ptah: The Craftsman Creator of Memphis

If Ra created through power and Amun through hidden force, Ptah created through craft and thought. He was the patron god of craftsmen, architects, and artists. He was Memphis's supreme deity. And in Memphis theology, he was the ultimate creator who had made even the other gods.

Ptah appeared as a man wrapped tightly in a white shroud, standing on a platform and holding a staff that combined three powerful symbols: the ankh (life), the djed (stability), and the was (power). His tight wrapping resembled a mummy, connecting him to death and transformation, though he was very much a god of creation and life.

Memphis was Egypt's first capital, located where the Nile Delta begins, strategically positioned between Upper and Lower Egypt. Being Memphis's patron god made Ptah one of Egypt's most important deities, regardless of changing political fortunes.

According to Memphis theology, preserved on the Shabaka Stone, Ptah created the universe through thought and speech. He conceived of creation in his heart—the Egyptians believed the heart was the organ of thought—and spoke it into existence with his tongue.

This is remarkably similar to the biblical "Let there be light" creation. In fact, the Memphis creation account predates Genesis by well over a thousand years. The idea that speaking something makes it real and that words have creative power appeared first in Ptah's myth.

Ptah's most important role was as patron of craftsmen. Every sculptor, architect, goldsmith, carpenter, and artisan honored Ptah. Before beginning work, craftsmen made offerings to him. His priests included master craftsmen who trained apprentices in sacred techniques.

The Egyptians took craftsmanship seriously. Objects were not just functional. They were imbued with divine creative energy. A well-made statue, piece of jewelry, or carved relief used the same creative force that Ptah had used to make the universe. This was why Egyptian art maintained such high standards for so long.

Ptah's wife was Sekhmet, the lion-headed destroyer goddess. Their son was Nefertem, a lotus god associated with perfume and beauty. The three formed the Memphis Triad, paralleling the Theban Triad of Amun, Mut, and Khonsu. These divine families represented completeness, with male creative power, female protective power, and youthful renewal.

Ptah's temple at Memphis was one of Egypt's grandest, though less survives today than at Karnak. Ancient writers described it as magnificent, filled with masterwork statues and reliefs. Pharaohs commissioned additions to Ptah's temple throughout Egyptian history, each trying to outdo predecessors in craftsmanship and beauty.

One interesting thing is that Ptah was associated with the Apis bull. Apis was a sacred bull kept at Memphis, and it was worshiped as a living manifestation of Ptah. Only one Apis bull existed at a time. It had to have specific markings: black with a white triangular marking on the forehead, a crescent-moon shape on its side, and other distinctive features. When an Apis bull died, priests searched all of Egypt for the next bull with the correct markings. When found, it was brought to Memphis with great ceremony and installed in the temple.

The Apis bull lived in luxury, as it was fed choice food and tended by priests. When it died, it was mummified and buried in the Serapeum, underground galleries containing massive sarcophagi for the Apis bulls. These burials were elaborate, expensive funerals.

Ptah demonstrated that creation was not just about power. It was about intelligence, planning, and skilled execution. Ra might provide energy, but Ptah provided design. Both were necessary for a functioning universe.

Mut and Khonsu: Completing the Theban Triad

Amun did not rule alone. He had a divine family: his wife, Mut, and their son, Khonsu. Together, they formed the Theban Triad, the three gods honored at Karnak.

Mut's name meant "mother." She was the ultimate divine mother, representing maternal protection, queenship, and the fierce loyalty mothers show when defending their children.

She appeared as a woman wearing a vulture headdress and the double crown of Upper and Lower Egypt. The vulture connected her to Nekhbet, the protective vulture goddess of Upper Egypt. The double crown marked her as queen of the gods, Amun's equal in authority. Queens of Egypt were associated with Mut just as kings were associated with Amun. Sometimes, Mut appeared with a lioness head, connecting her to Sekhmet.

Mut nursing Pharaoh Seti I.[19]

Her temple at Karnak, though smaller than Amun's, was still impressive. A sacred lake surrounded part of it and was used for ritual purification. Priests raised and bred cats at Mut's temple. Mummified cats from Mut's temple show that she was honored through these sacred animals.

Mut's annual festival involved carrying her statue to meet Amun's statue, symbolically renewing their divine marriage and ensuring cosmic fertility. These ritual marriages between god and goddess statues occurred throughout Egypt. They were not merely symbolic. The Egyptians believed the gods genuinely inhabited their statues during festivals and that these ritual unions had real effects on the world.

Khonsu was the son of Amun and Mut. He was the moon god, though Thoth also had lunar associations. Khonsu's name meant "Traveler" because the moon travels across the night sky.

Khonsu appeared as a young man with a sidelock of youth, a hairstyle showing he was still a child or adolescent. He wore the moon disk on his head, often with a crescent moon incorporated into the design. He carried a crook and flail like Osiris. He also sometimes appears with a falcon or hawk head.

As the moon god, Khonsu controlled time. The lunar calendar was essential for religious festivals, agricultural planning, and administrative purposes. Khonsu marked the passage of months through the moon's phases. He was "Khonsu the Reckoner," counting and measuring time's passage.

Khonsu also had healing powers. One famous text describes how Khonsu's statue was sent to a foreign land to heal a princess possessed by demons. The statue successfully exorcised the demons, proving that Khonsu's power extended beyond Egypt.

His temple at Karnak still stands and is one of the best-preserved parts of the complex. Built by Ramesses III, it demonstrates New Kingdom architectural style at its finest. The temple had its own sacred barque for carrying Khonsu's statue during festivals and its own priesthood.

The Theban Triad represented complete divine authority: the father, Amun, as creator and king; the mother, Mut, as protector and queen; and the son, Khonsu, as heir and continuer of divine power. This family structure mirrored the human family and the royal family, showing that all families operated on the same principles, just at different scales.

Families came to Karnak to pray before all three gods. They prayed to Amun for success and prosperity, to Mut for protection of children and family, and to Khonsu for healing, safe travels, and favorable passage of time. The Triad covered everything a family needed from the gods.

Neith: The Ancient Warrior and Weaver

Neith was ancient even by Egyptian standards. She appeared in the earliest dynasties, as her symbols have been found on artifacts from the very beginning of Egyptian civilization. She was older than Ra and Osiris. And she never lost importance throughout Egypt's three-thousand-year history.

Her main cult center was Sais in the western Nile Delta. Sais was one of Egypt's most ancient cities. Neith was its patron, protector, and supreme deity. During Egypt's later periods, Sais became the capital several times, elevating Neith's importance even further.

Neith appeared as a woman wearing the Red Crown of Lower Egypt, carrying a bow and two arrows or holding a weaving shuttle. These symbols captured her dual nature as destroyer and creator.

As a warrior goddess, Neith protected Egypt from enemies. She carried a bow, which was unusual for Egyptian goddesses, who usually used other weapons or magic. The bow made her a goddess of hunters and soldiers. Pharaohs invoked Neith before battles, asking her to guide their arrows and ensure victory.

Neith was also a weaver. She wove the world itself, creating the universe through the act of weaving threads together. Taking separate threads and combining them into a unified cloth mirrored how creation brought together separate elements into an ordered cosmos.

Neith's most famous titles were "Neith the Great" and "the Mother of Gods." She was the beginning of everything, the first being who existed before existence, and the mother who bore the gods themselves.

Different myths gave different accounts of Neith's role in creation. Memphis theology, Ptah's version, did not emphasize her role. Heliopolis theology, Ra's version, did not either. However, Sais theology insisted that Neith came first. She wove the world, gave birth to Ra, and created the first gods. Everything else descended from her. The Egyptians never resolved these competing claims about who created what first.

During *The Contendings of Horus and Set* (which we discussed in Chapter 3), Neith was consulted as a wise mediator. The tribunal sent her a letter asking her opinion on who deserved the throne. Neith responded that Horus should rule Egypt but that Set should receive compensation. Her wisdom helped resolve the dispute.

Neith was also associated with death and funerary rites. She helped protect the deceased in the underworld. She used her weaving skills to create the burial shrouds that wrapped mummies. Some funerary texts described Neith as helping Isis and Nephthys protect Osiris's body after Set murdered him.

Her temple at Sais was magnificent, though little survives today. Ancient writers described it as one of Egypt's most important religious sites. The Greek historian Herodotus visited Sais and described Neith's festival as one of Egypt's grandest celebrations, involving lights and processions.

Greeks identified Neith with Athena, their warrior goddess of wisdom and crafts. The comparison was apt. Both were fierce warrior goddesses associated with weaving and wisdom. Both protected their cities—Neith protected Sais, and Athena protected Athens. Both gave strategic advice in conflicts. The overlap made Neith one of the Egyptian deities that the Greeks most easily understood and adopted.

Late Period pharaohs, particularly those of the Saite dynasty (664–525 BCE), emphasized Neith's importance. Sais was their capital, and they promoted her worship as part of asserting their legitimacy. They claimed Neith's ancient authority to legitimize their relatively new dynasty.

Neith remained important from the very first dynasty to the final days of the Egyptian religion. Gods rose and fell in prominence. Political capitals changed. Foreign powers conquered Egypt. However, Neith endured.

Min: God of Fertility, Virility, and Desert Roads

Min was impossible to miss. He stood upright, arm raised high, with an enormously erect phallus. His artistic depictions were explicit and unapologetic. He was the god of male sexuality, fertility, and reproduction, and the Egyptians celebrated rather than hid these aspects. Male fertility was essential for human survival, agricultural abundance, and the continuation of family lines.

Min's main cult centers were Akhmim and Koptos in Upper Egypt. Both were ancient cities where Min had been worshiped since the earliest dynasties. Koptos was particularly important because it was the starting point for trade routes into the Eastern Desert and the Red Sea, connecting Egypt with foreign lands and luxury goods.

Min was the god of desert travelers, caravan leaders, and miners. The Eastern Desert was dangerous; it was hot, waterless, and full of raiders and

A relief of Min at the Karnak temple complex.[20]

wild animals. However, it also contained valuable resources, like gold, precious stones, and access to trade routes. Travelers heading into the desert prayed to Min for protection and safe passage.

His role as a desert god is connected symbolically to his sexuality. The desert was harsh and barren. Min's fertility power counteracted that barrenness, blessing travelers with success and bringing them safely back to the fertile Nile Valley. He represented life and abundance, opposing the desert's death and scarcity.

Min was associated with Amun. Sometimes, they merged as Min-Amun or Amun-Min, combining Min's fertility with Amun's creative power. This connection made sense since both gods represented generative force. Amun was the hidden creative principle, and Min was that principle made physically and sexually manifest.

Lettuce was sacred to Min. Recall from Chapter 3 how lettuce played a role in the Horus and Set story. Lettuce's milky sap resembled semen, connecting it to male sexuality and fertility. Min's festivals involved offerings of lettuce. His priests ate lettuce ceremonially, and fields dedicated to Min grew lettuce specifically for temple use.

The Festival of Min was one of Egypt's most important celebrations. The pharaoh participated personally, demonstrating his own vitality and ability to father heirs. During the festival, the pharaoh cut grain with a sickle, symbolically ensuring the harvest's fertility through his connection to Min.

Min's sexuality was not about personal pleasure, though the Egyptians did not condemn that either. It was about biological and agricultural necessity. Sex created children. Children continued family lines, worked fields, and cared for elderly parents. Abundant sexuality meant abundant life, which meant survival and prosperity.

Bulls were sacred to Min, representing male sexual power and fertility. Black bulls in particular were associated with him. His priests maintained sacred bull herds. When pharaohs performed ritual bull hunts or bull sacrifices, they demonstrated mastery over Min's wild, powerful sexual energy while also honoring it.

Women prayed to Min for help in conceiving children. Couples hoping for fertility made offerings at his temples. Men concerned about virility invoked Min's aid.

Min also represented the productive power of physical labor. His raised arm holding a flail symbolized the strength needed for farming, mining, and building. Fertility was not just sexual; it was also about the body's ability to work, create, and produce abundance through physical effort.

Greeks and Romans continued to honor Min, sometimes under the name "Pan" because of superficial similarities to their own fertility god. His worship persisted longer than that of many other Egyptian deities because fertility gods remained relevant regardless of political changes or cultural shifts. Everyone needed crops to grow and children to be born.

Min represented life itself—raw, powerful, unashamed, necessary life. He was essential because the continuation of life was essential.

Chapter 5: Geography of the Dead

The Soul's Many Parts: Ba, Ka, Akh, and More

Death wasn't simple for the Egyptians. When someone died, they didn't just have one "soul" that went to heaven or hell. Instead, the person split into multiple components, each with its own purpose and destination.

The most important components were the ba, the ka, and the akh. But there were others too, such as the shadow (shut), the name (ren), and the physical body itself. These beliefs about different soul parts grew more complex over time. In the Old Kingdom, Egyptians focused mainly on the body and ka. Later, they added more parts to the picture, creating the detailed system we're describing here.

Let's start with the ka.

The ka was your life force, your vital energy. It was created when you were born. Khnum, as we discussed in Chapter 4, was sometimes depicted fashioning the ka on his potter's wheel alongside your physical body. The ka was what made you alive.

The ka needed sustenance. This is why Egyptians left offerings at tombs like bread, beer, meat, wine, and fruit. These offerings fed the ka. Without them, the ka would starve and cease to exist.

The ka's hieroglyph was two upraised arms, representing embrace and protection. Your ka was like your spiritual double, existing parallel to your physical body throughout life and continuing after death.

When someone died, the ka separated from the body. It lived in the tomb. Tombs were designed as eternal homes. It had decorated rooms with furniture, supplies, and artwork showing the deceased enjoying food and drink.

Next, the ba.

The ba was closer to what we might call personality or soul. It was your individual essence—what made you specifically you. Your memories, your character, your emotions, and your identity were all part of the ba.

The ba was depicted as a human-headed bird, usually a falcon or hawk with a person's face. This form made sense. The ba could move around freely, flying between the tomb and the outside world. Unlike the ka, which stayed in the tomb, the ba could travel.

A golden ba amulet.[21]

During the day, the ba could leave the tomb and visit familiar places. It might fly to the deceased's house, visit the Nile, or enjoy the sunshine. According to some texts, the ba needed to return to the tomb and reunite with the mummified body regularly.

The ba needed a body to return to. If the body decayed beyond recognition, the ba might not recognize it and could become lost. The preserved mummy served as an anchor, ensuring the ba could always find its way home.

Now the akh.

The akh was the transfigured spirit, the perfected form—what you became if everything went right. Not everyone became an akh. You had to earn it through righteous living, proper burial, and successfully navigating the afterlife's challenges.

The akh's hieroglyph was a crested ibis (a different bird than the ibis form of Thoth). In art, the akh might be shown as a human figure glowing with light or radiance. The word "akh" is related to "effectiveness" and "light."

An akh was no longer constrained by mortality's limitations. The akh lived with the gods and the stars. It sailed with Ra on his solar boat and dwelt in the Field of Reeds, the paradise of the afterlife. The akh achieved what every Egyptian hoped for—immortality in a perfected state.

The relationship between ba, ka, and akh wasn't a simple formula. Egyptian texts described the process poetically rather than mechanically. The ba and ka needed to be maintained properly, the body had to be preserved, the proper rituals needed to be performed, and divine judgment had to be passed. It wasn't automatic. Death didn't make you an akh. You had to work for it, and you needed help from the living (through offerings and rituals) and from the gods (through divine judgment and magic).

The shadow (shut) was another component. Your shadow wasn't just the dark shape cast by your body. It was a spiritual element and a part of your identity. The shadow was an aspect of being, tied to your presence and existence in the world.

Why did shadows matter? Well, they were evidence of your existence. Only things that exist cast shadows. A person without a shadow would be incomplete, not fully real. The shadow represented your presence in the world and your ability to interact with physical space.

The name (ren) was perhaps the most important component of all. Your name was your identity. To speak someone's name was to make them exist. To forget someone's name was to erase them from existence. Tomb inscriptions repeated the deceased's name over and over, as speaking the name kept the person existing.

The worst punishment imaginable was having your name destroyed. If your name was chiseled off monuments, erased from records, and forgotten by everyone, you ceased to exist entirely. This was worse than death. This was obliteration. Some pharaohs deliberately erased the names of predecessors they hated, trying to destroy them retroactively.

Knowing the true names of gods and demons gave you power over them. Names weren't just labels. They were also the essence of identity. Your name was you in the deepest sense.

The physical body was also very important. The body was the anchor for all the other components. The ba needed to return to it to maintain connection. The ka needed it to remain recognizable. Offerings were made to it. The body was the center around which the afterlife was organized.

The heart (ib) had special importance. While modern people think of the brain as the seat of thought and identity, Egyptians believed the heart was where thinking, memory, and moral character resided. The brain was considered unimportant and was removed during mummification. However, the heart stayed in the body because it would be needed for judgment.

In the Hall of Two Truths, where Osiris judged the dead, the heart was weighed against the feather of Ma'at. The heart testified to how you'd lived. If it were heavy with sin, you'd fail judgment. If it were light and pure, you'd pass. Your heart literally determined your fate.

The living had responsibilities to the dead. You had to provide offerings for the ka, speak the name to sustain the ren, maintain the tomb so the ba had somewhere to return, and ensure proper mummification so the body remained intact. Failing in these duties meant your relatives couldn't achieve eternal life.

Family tombs were common. Tomb chapels had offering tables and false doors, magic portals between the living world and the tomb. The living and the dead maintained relationships. Death separated you physically, but proper religious practice kept familial connections alive.

The Journey Through the Duat: Perils, Demons, and Magic

Death was just the beginning. After dying, the deceased faced a dangerous journey through the Duat, the Egyptian underworld. It was a realm everyone had to traverse to reach the afterlife. The Duat was dark, filled with demons and challenges, but navigable with the right knowledge.

The Duat existed somewhere beneath the earth and simultaneously in a supernatural realm outside normal space. Ra traveled through it every night on his solar boat. The dead also traveled through it, following pathways, passing through gates, and encountering strange beings. The journey took time. How much time varied depending on the text, but it wasn't instant.

Multiple texts described the Duat, and they didn't always agree. The Book of the Dead (which the Egyptians called "Spells of Coming Forth by Day") was the most famous collection of spells to help the deceased navigate the afterlife. But there were also the Pyramid Texts (the oldest religious texts in the world, carved inside Old Kingdom pyramids), the Coffin Texts (written on Middle Kingdom coffins), the Book of Gates, the Book of Caverns, and others.

Each text emphasized different aspects of the journey and used different imagery, but common themes appeared across all of them: darkness, gates requiring knowledge or magical words, demons that needed to be convinced or defeated, transformations, and the final judgment before Osiris.

The journey began the moment you died. Your ba separated from your body. You found yourself in darkness. According to the texts, the first challenge was knowing what to do next. Having knowledge of spells and magical formulas greatly increased your chances of success.

The wealthy paid for copies of the Book of the Dead to be buried with them. These papyrus scrolls contained spells, guidance, and instructions for navigating the Duat. Each spell had a specific purpose, such as transforming into different animals, passing through gates, defeating demons, finding water, avoiding hazards, and proving your worthiness.

Different texts described the Duat's geography differently. The Amduat organized it into twelve regions representing the twelve hours of night. The Book of the Dead presented a more loosely connected series of challenges and locations. There was no single official map, but common features appeared across texts. Some regions were burning deserts. Others were flooded with water. Some had pits of fire. Others had walls of iron. The deceased had to navigate these hazards successfully.

Gates blocked the way. These weren't ordinary gates. They were magical barriers guarded by demons and gods. Many texts describe gates requiring the right spell or knowledge to pass. The gatekeeper might demand, "What is your name? What is this gate's name? Who guards this threshold?" Knowing the answers or having the right magical formula could allow passage.

Demons roamed the Duat. They had names like "He Who Dances in Blood" and "Breaker of Bones." The spells provided ways to defend against them. These magical words paralyzed demons or transformed the deceased into forms they couldn't attack.

The Book of the Dead contained numerous transformation spells. These let the deceased transform into different animals and objects, including a phoenix, a lotus, a falcon, a crocodile, and even gold. The

Egyptians believed you could take on the powers of these forms. For instance, one could gain the speed of a falcon, the resilience of gold, or the regenerative power of a lotus.

Water was essential. The Duat had incredibly dry regions. Finding water kept you existing. Some spells created water where there was none. Others led you to wells or rivers. Without water, you'd dry up and cease to exist, leading to a "second death" that meant permanent obliteration.

You also needed to find Osiris. The ultimate goal was reaching the Hall of Two Truths, where Osiris sat in judgment. But finding it required navigating successfully through the Duat's dangerous regions.

The deceased wasn't alone in the Duat. Anubis served as a guide for some. Your ba, if it had successfully left the tomb, accompanied you. Sometimes, family members who had died before you might help. But you mainly relied on magical knowledge and your own virtue to succeed.

One particularly dangerous section was called the Lake of Fire. This was a region of burning water. The water was somehow also fire, and it was hot enough to destroy the unworthy. Only those who had passed certain tests could cross it safely. Some texts describe boats that could sail on the Lake of Fire, but you had to know the boat's name and the boatman's name to be allowed aboard.

The Duat had its own inhabitants who lived there permanently. Not all were hostile. Some gods maintained order in the Duat, punishing demons and helping the justified dead. But you had to know whom to trust and whom to avoid. A being might appear helpful but actually be a trap. The spells provided guidance on identifying friends from foes.

Time worked strangely in the Duat. The journey might feel like days or years, but to the living world, no time passed at all. You existed in a liminal space between life and death, between existence and nonexistence.

The wealthy dead had advantages. Their tombs contained detailed maps and guides. Their mummies were buried with amulets providing magical protection. They had servants (shabtis, magical figurines that would perform labor in the afterlife) to help with any work required. The poor had fewer resources and probably had more difficulty completing the journey.

However, virtue mattered more than wealth in the end. The final judgment before Osiris evaluated your character, not your possessions. A righteous poor person could succeed where a wicked rich person would fail.

Eventually, after passing through all the regions and surviving all the challenges, you reached the Hall of Two Truths.

The Weighing of the Heart: Judgment Before Osiris

The Hall of Two Truths was where everything was decided. This was the courtroom of the afterlife, the place where your heart was weighed against truth itself.

Osiris sat on his throne. He wore the white crown, held the crook and flail, and appeared as a mummified king. He was the ultimate judge. His word was final. Around him stood the Ennead and other gods. They witnessed the judgment but did not interfere. This was Osiris's domain.

Anubis was present, operating the scales. Thoth stood ready to record the results with his writing palette and stylus. Ma'at herself might be present or just her feather—the ultimate symbol of truth, justice, and cosmic order.

And there, in the corner, lurked Ammit the Devourer.

Ammit was nightmare made flesh. She was a monster with a crocodile's head, a lion's forequarters, and a hippopotamus's hindquarters. These were the three most dangerous animals in Egypt, combined into one terrifying being. Ammit didn't judge. She simply waited. If your heart was found wanting, she ate it. And eating your heart meant you ceased to exist permanently.

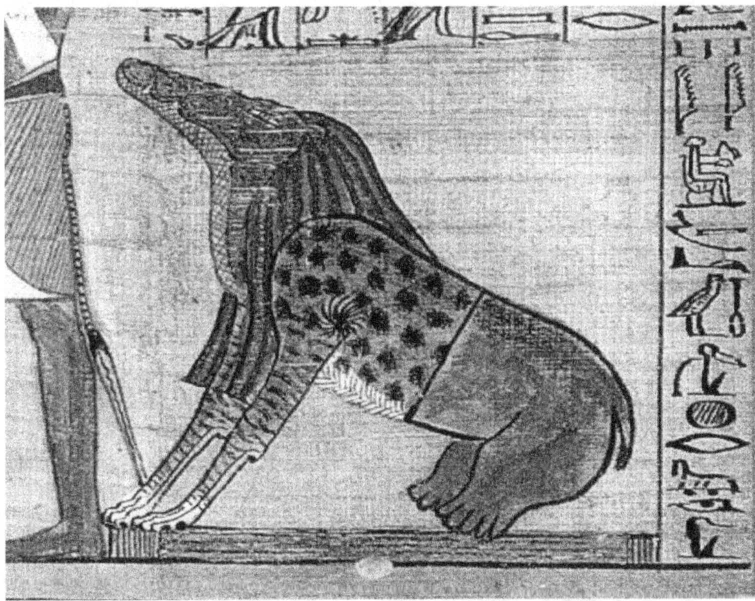

Ammit depicted in the Papyrus of Ani, c. 1250 BCE.[22]

You entered the Hall of Two Truths. The journey through the Duat was over. Now came the final test. Everything depended on what happened next.

The first part of the judgment was the Negative Confession. You had to stand before the forty-two divine assessors (one for each of Egypt's forty-two administrative districts) and declare all the sins you hadn't committed.

"I have not killed." "I have not stolen." "I have not lied." "I have not committed adultery." "I have not been angry without cause." "I have not polluted water." "I have not been proud." "I have not been greedy."

The confession continued. This wasn't claiming you were perfect; it was claiming you hadn't committed serious violations of Ma'at. The list covered major moral offenses that would disqualify you from eternal life.

The declarations had to be truthful. You couldn't lie before the gods. Your heart knew the truth, and your heart was about to testify.

After the Negative Confession, Anubis brought the scales forward. These weren't ordinary scales. They were the scales of truth, perfectly balanced and incapable of error. On one side of the scale, Anubis placed your heart. On the other side, he placed the feather of Ma'at.

The feather was small and light. It represented truth, justice, and right living. If your heart was lighter than or equal to the feather, you had lived according to Ma'at. If your heart was heavier than the feather, you had been corrupted by sin and selfishness.

Everyone watched. The gods. Osiris. Your ba watching from outside your body. The scales moved. Would the heart be light enough?

The texts don't describe how long this took. It probably felt like forever. Your entire existence depended on this moment. Everything you'd been in life, every choice you'd made, every act of kindness or cruelty—all of it was being measured against that single feather.

If your heart balanced perfectly with the feather, Anubis announced the result. Thoth recorded it in his eternal records. Osiris proclaimed you "justified" or "true of voice" (*maa-kheru* in Egyptian). You had passed. You were worthy of eternal life.

Anubis then led you to Osiris. You approached the throne. Osiris might speak to you, welcoming you to the afterlife. Or he might simply nod, confirming the judgment. Either way, you had succeeded. You would live forever.

But if your heart was heavy...

The scales tipped. The heart weighed more than the feather. The sin and wrongdoing from your life had weighed down your heart. Thoth recorded this result too. Anubis stepped back. And Ammit moved forward.

She devoured your heart whole. And with your heart gone, you ceased to exist. You had already died, so this wasn't death as we know it. Rather, this was the second death, the final death, the death from which there was no return.

The texts don't dwell on this fate. Those who failed judgment simply vanished from existence. They didn't suffer eternal torment. They weren't punished forever. They simply stopped being. There was no afterlife for them. They would have no memory or legacy.

Some wealthy people sought additional insurance. They buried themselves with spells to help their heart in judgment. The heart scarab, a large scarab amulet placed over the heart during mummification, was inscribed with a spell from the Book of the Dead. This spell was essentially a plea asking the heart to be truthful and kind in its testimony and not to make the deceased look worse than they were.

The weighing of the heart was the climax of the entire afterlife. Everything before it—the mummification, the offerings, the journey through the Duat—was preparation. Everything after it—eternal life in paradise—was the reward. That single moment determined everything.

The weighing of the heart meant Egyptians cared deeply about how you lived your life. Your afterlife wasn't determined by performing the right rituals (though those helped), or paying the right priests (though that helped too), or being born into the right family (though that gave advantages). Ultimately, your afterlife depended on how you'd lived. A pharaoh and a merchant faced the same judgment before the same scales.

This doesn't mean Egyptian society was perfectly just or that everyone was treated fairly in life. It wasn't, and they weren't. But the belief that everyone faced the same divine judgment after death provided a powerful incentive for ethical behavior and gave ordinary people a sense that cosmic justice existed, even if earthly justice was often lacking.

The Field of Reeds: Eternal Life in Paradise

The Field of Reeds (Aaru in Egyptian, also called the Field of Offerings) was one vision of the afterlife that many Egyptians hoped to reach. This was paradise for those who lived according to Ma'at and successfully navigated death's challenges.

It's important to note that Egyptian afterlife beliefs weren't uniform. The Osirian afterlife (judgment and the Field of Reeds) coexisted with solar afterlife traditions (sailing with Ra) and stellar traditions (becoming stars). These different visions existed side by side and sometimes blended together. The Egyptians weren't worried about having one consistent story, the way we might be today. A person might hope to dwell in the Field of Reeds and sail with Ra and shine as a star. However, we'll focus here on the Field of Reeds tradition since it became the most widespread.

This paradise wasn't some abstract spiritual realm. It was a physical place with geography, crops, and activities. The Egyptians imagined the afterlife as an idealized version of Egypt itself. It was supposed to be the best parts of earthly life, perfected and made eternal.

The Field of Reeds was located in the east, where the sun rose. It existed in or near the Duat but was a separate, blessed region. Some texts described it as islands in a divine river. Others described it as fields extending endlessly under perfect blue skies. The details varied, but the essential image remained the same: a beautiful, fertile, peaceful land where everything was abundant.

What did the Field of Reeds look like?

Imagine Egypt during the best season, after the Nile's flood had receded, leaving rich black soil. Fields of grain grow tall and healthy. Fruit trees are heavy with dates and figs. Canals are full of clean water. The weather is perfect—not too hot, never cold. There are no droughts. No crop failures. No disease. No violence. No death.

Grain grows taller than any earthly grain. Harvests are always abundant. Food is plentiful and delicious. The water is pure and refreshing. This was paradise tailored specifically for agricultural people who'd spent their lives worrying about floods, droughts, and crop failures.

Paradise wasn't a place of endless leisure. You had to plow fields, plant grain, harvest crops, maintain irrigation canals, and perform all the agricultural labor that life in Egypt required. The difference was that the work was always successful and always rewarded. You'd plow and plant, and crops would grow perfectly. You'd harvest, and there'd be more than enough. The work was satisfying rather than exhausting.

A depiction of the Field of Reeds from c. 1775 BCE.[28]

This was where shabtis came in. Remember those? They were small figurines, often mummiform (shaped like mummies), that were buried with the dead. Sometimes, a tomb would have dozens or even hundreds of them. Why?

Shabtis were magical servants who would do work for you in the afterlife. When called to labor, you could send your shabti in your place. Wealthy people had shabtis for every day of the year, plus overseer shabtis to manage the workers.

The shabtis had spells inscribed on them, such as Spell 6 from the Book of the Dead. "If I am called to do work in paradise, you shall do it for me." The poor probably had to do their own work, though the texts suggest the work wasn't burdensome.

What else did people do there?

They spent time with family members who'd died before them. They saw friends and relatives, renewing relationships that death had interrupted. The social bonds of life continued in the afterlife.

They ate and drank, not because they needed sustenance—they were spirits now—but because eating and drinking brought pleasure. Offerings from the living world appeared in the Field of Reeds, adding to the abundance already present. All the good things the living left at tombs—bread, beer, meat, and wine—materialized in the afterlife for the deceased to enjoy.

They participated in festivals. The afterlife had celebrations, religious observances, and communal gatherings just like in life. These festivals honored the gods and reinforced the community of the blessed dead. Death didn't mean isolation from social life; it meant joining a larger community of successful souls.

They could also sail with Ra on his solar boat. This was a special honor. The akh—the transfigured spirit—could join Ra's crew during his daily and nightly journey. You'd help defend against Apep, assist in maintaining cosmic order, and participate in the rhythm of creation.

Some texts describe how the deceased could visit the living world during certain festivals or on certain days. Your ba could leave paradise and fly back to Egypt, visiting your old home, checking on your family, and enjoying familiar sights. You maintained a connection with the world of the living even while dwelling in the afterlife.

Paradise was eternal. You couldn't die again. You couldn't get sick. You couldn't age or decline. You existed in a perfect state forever.

This paradise represented what the Egyptians valued most: abundance, community, meaningful work, connection to the gods, and security. It wasn't a place of clouds and harps. It was distinctly Egyptian.

For the Egyptians, this vision of the afterlife made death less terrifying. Yes, dying was frightening. Yes, the journey through the Duat was dangerous. Yes, judgment was nerve-wracking. But beyond all that lay paradise, where you could live forever in the best possible version of the life you'd known.

Chapter 6: Magic, Monsters, and Mayhem

Heka: The Magic That Made the Universe

The word "heka" meant both magic itself and the god who personified it. Heka was the power that created the universe, sustained it, and allowed gods and humans to accomplish anything beyond normal means.

The god Heka was sometimes depicted as a man holding two serpents, representing the dual nature of magic. According to Egyptian belief, Heka existed before creation. When nothing else existed, Heka was already there in the primordial waters of Nu. Heka was the force Atum used to speak creation into being. Without Heka, nothing could exist or function. Some texts call Heka the Ka of Ra since magic was the sun god's life force.

Magic wasn't opposing the natural order. Magic *was* the natural order. The sun rising each morning? That required heka. Crops growing? Healing from illness? All heka. The boundary between "natural" and "magical" didn't exist the way modern people think of it. Everything involved heka to some degree.

Magical belief was widespread across Egyptian society, though knowledge and skill varied by education, profession, and access to texts. Mothers spoke protective spells over their children. Farmers used magic to protect crops from pests. Workers wore amulets to prevent accidents. Doctors combined medicine with magical incantations. Professional magicians weren't special because they had magic; everyone had access to magical practices. They were just better at it, like any other skilled trade.

Egyptian magic worked in several ways. Words were powerful. Speaking the right words in the right way could make things happen. Some rituals emphasized exact wording, while others allowed variation in everyday practice. Many formal spells began with "Words to be spoken" and gave precise instructions for pronunciation and delivery.

But speaking wasn't enough if you didn't know what to call things. Names had power too. Knowing something's true name gave you power over it. This applied to gods, demons, people, animals, and objects. Remember in Chapter 2 when Isis learned Ra's secret name and gained power over him? Spells listed names of demons, gates, and gods specifically because speaking the name invoked or controlled that being.

Written words had their own power. Hieroglyphs were called *medu netjer* ("words of the gods"). Writing something down made it real and permanent. This is why tomb inscriptions depicted food, drink, and offerings. The images themselves had magical power and could sustain the ka even if physical offerings stopped coming.

Words and names needed to be accompanied by the right actions. Magic often required physical gestures, materials, or ritual actions, such as tying knots while reciting spells or drawing protective symbols on doorways. The physical action, combined with the spoken spell, created the magical effect.

Timing mattered too. Magic was performed at significant times such as dawn, festivals, or auspicious days. Egyptian magicians kept careful track of calendars to know when magic would be most effective.

The most powerful magic combined everything. A healing spell might require speaking the words correctly, writing them on papyrus, dissolving the papyrus in water, drinking the water, wearing an amulet, and performing the ritual at dawn during a specific phase of the moon. The more elements one combined properly, the more powerful the magic.

Priests were professional magicians. Their training included memorizing hundreds of spells, learning proper pronunciation, understanding timing and materials, and mastering rituals. The "lector priest" (*hery-heb* in Egyptian) was responsible for reciting spells during rituals. These priests were experts in heka, carrying scrolls of spells and performing magic on behalf of temples and clients.

The House of Life (Per Ankh) was attached to temples and served as a library, scriptorium, medical school, and magic academy. Sacred texts were stored, copied, and studied there, including magical texts alongside medical, astronomical, and religious writings. The House of Life trained scribes and priests in reading, writing, and magical knowledge.

However, magic wasn't limited to official priests. There were also lay magicians, people who practiced magic professionally without being temple priests. Some were healers, combining medical knowledge with magical spells. Others were diviners who could see the future or find lost objects. Some specialized in protective magic, creating amulets and performing rituals to guard against dangers. A few practiced harmful magic, like cursing enemies, causing illness, or disrupting someone's life, though this was officially condemned and could be punished.

The famous Harem Conspiracy during the reign of Ramesses III shows this wasn't theoretical. Conspirators created wax figurines and used magic to try to harm or kill the pharaoh. They were caught, tried, and executed, showing that magical crimes were taken seriously and treated as real threats rather than superstitious nonsense.

Egyptian literary tales describe "magic wars" between competing magicians. The famous story of Khaemwaset (a prince and magician) tells of magical duels where opponents transformed into animals, cast spells at each other, and tried to out-magic their rivals. These stories were entertainment and mythology rather than accounts of real magical practice, but they show how Egyptians imagined magical power at its most dramatic.

Foreign magic was acknowledged but considered inferior or dangerous. Egyptian magic was the oldest and most powerful. It came from the gods and had been practiced since creation. Foreign magicians might have tricks, but Egyptian magic had divine authority. However, Egyptian magical practice did absorb elements from other cultures over time, especially during periods of foreign contact and rule.

Magic pervaded Egyptian life from birth to death and beyond. Before birth, magic protected pregnant women and helped ensure a safe delivery. At birth, magic defended the infant from demons that threatened newborns. Through life, magic provided protection, healing, and prosperity. At death, magic preserved the body, guided the soul, and ensured eternal life. For Egyptians, magic was how you made things happen.

Apep: The Serpent of Chaos

We've mentioned Apep several times already, but he deserves more attention, as he was perhaps the most dangerous being in Egyptian mythology. Apep (also called Apophis in Greek) was a gigantic serpent thousands of cubits long who attacked Ra's solar boat every night. He was the embodiment of chaos and tried to unmake the universe.

The nightly battle was crucial. Set stood at the prow with his spear, defending Ra. Other defenders included Mehen (a serpent god who coiled protectively around Ra's cabin) and sometimes deceased pharaohs who had joined Ra's eternal journey.

Set would spear Apep repeatedly. The serpent would bleed; myths said red dawn skies were Apep's blood. He would scream and writhe. Magical spells weakened him, and fire burned him. The combined assault drove him back.

But Apep could never be killed permanently. The next night, he'd return, just as dangerous as ever.

When eclipses occurred, Egyptians understood this as Apep temporarily succeeding. Priests performed emergency rituals—the "Repelling of Apep" ceremony—to help Ra escape.

The Book of Overthrowing Apep was a collection of spells and rituals designed to combat the chaos serpent. It described his appearance, nature, weaknesses, and the magic needed to defeat him. Temples performed these rituals regularly as preventive magic.

Some rituals involved creating wax or clay figurines of Apep and then ritually stabbing, burning, or breaking them while reciting spells. This harmed the actual Apep.

Apep had followers and allies—demons and hostile beings who sided with chaos against Ma'at. These demons assisted Apep or caused their own chaos.

The serpent's eyes held great power. Texts emphasize the terror of Apep's gaze and warn against confronting him directly. Some protective spells included phrases about not looking at Apep or becoming immune to his eyes' power.

Despite being the ultimate enemy, Apep unified everyone against a common threat. He constantly endangered Egyptian society through drought, famine, disease, and foreign invasion. He gave purpose to Set's violence and made the daily sunrise meaningful rather than automatic.

Apep represented the threat that chaos was always near and gave it a face that the Egyptians could fight.

The Destruction of Mankind

This myth is less well known than some others, but it's important for understanding how Egyptians viewed the relationship between gods and humanity and how they explained the current state of the world. It also features Sekhmet in her most terrifying role.

The story begins with Ra ruling as the king of both gods and humans. This was at the beginning of time, when gods walked the earth and pharaohs weren't needed yet because Ra himself governed everything directly.

But Ra grew old. Even gods aged in Egyptian thought. The texts use precious metals and stones to describe his aging. His bones became silver, his flesh gold, and his hair like lapis lazuli. He looked elderly and fragile.

Humanity, which Ra had created, saw his aging and began to disrespect him. They mocked his appearance and stopped following his commands. They even plotted rebellion. Some versions suggest that humans planned to overthrow Ra and rule themselves, rejecting divine authority entirely.

This was isfet—chaos or rebellion against Ma'at. This was the created turning against their creator. Ra couldn't ignore it. Something had to be done.

Ra called a council of the great gods. He summoned Nu (the primordial water), Shu, Tefnut, Geb, Nut, and others who had existed since creation. He held this council secretly so humans wouldn't learn about it and flee.

Ra explained that humanity was planning to overthrow the divine order. What should he do?

The gods deliberated. They said humanity's rebellion couldn't be tolerated. Ma'at had to be restored. The created had to remember they served the creator. The gods advised Ra to send his Eye—his daughter and his fierce aspect—to punish humanity.

Ra agreed. He sent his Eye to earth in the form of Sekhmet, the lion-headed goddess of war and destruction.

Sekhmet descended to earth and began slaughtering humans. The texts describe her wading through blood, delighting in violence, crushing people under her feet, and tearing them apart with her claws. She killed thousands, tens of thousands. She killed indiscriminately too—rebels and innocents alike, old and young, guilty and blameless, all suffered at her hands.

This was divine retribution. This was what happened when Isfet (chaos and disorder) threatened Ma'at seriously enough to provoke the gods' direct intervention. This was the power of the divine unleashed without restraint.

The slaughter continued through the day. Sekhmet pursued humans wherever they fled. No one was safe. No one could hide. By evening, Egypt was soaked in blood. Bodies covered the ground. Survivors huddled in terror, expecting to die when morning came and Sekhmet resumed her massacre.

That night, Ra looked down at the carnage. He saw the blood and the bodies. He saw Sekhmet sleeping, exhausted from killing, ready to wake at dawn and continue the slaughter.

And Ra had second thoughts.

He'd wanted to punish humanity, to remind them who ruled, and to restore respect for divine authority. But destroying all of humanity would be excessive. It would undo part of creation. Humans were meant to exist. Ra himself had created them. Killing them all would be admitting his creation was a failure.

But Sekhmet was in a blood rage. She'd tasted human blood and loved it. She wouldn't stop just because Ra changed his mind. When morning came, she'd wake up and resume killing until every last human was dead.

Ra needed a plan—quickly.

He ordered his servants to gather large quantities of red ochre, a mineral that creates red pigment. He ordered them to gather barley and brew seven thousand jars' worth of beer. Then he ordered them to mix the red ochre into the beer, creating beer that looked exactly like blood.

Working through the night, the servants poured this blood-colored beer across the fields where Sekhmet would hunt at dawn. They flooded the area with it, creating what looked like a massive lake of blood.

Dawn came, and Sekhmet woke, ready for more killing. She saw the "blood" covering the fields and was delighted. So much blood! She bent down and began drinking.

She drank and drank. The beer tasted good. She drank thousands of jars' worth of beer-blood and got progressively drunker.

Eventually, Sekhmet passed out, completely intoxicated. When she woke, the bloodlust was gone. She had returned to her gentler aspect as Hathor, goddess of joy and love. Humanity was saved. They had been reduced in number, but they were saved.

Ra, seeing what had happened, decided he was done ruling directly. Humanity had proven itself troublesome. Governing humans was exhausting and led to situations like this. He would withdraw from his earthly rule.

Ra ordered Nut, the sky goddess, to transform into a cow and carry him up to the heavens. Nut became a celestial cow with Ra standing on her back, rising higher and higher until Ra reached the heavens far from earth.

The sky goddess Nut depicted as a cow.[34]

This myth explained a lot about the world the Egyptians lived in. The sun is far away in the heavens because Ra withdrew after humanity's rebellion. Gods don't walk the earth anymore because they returned to the divine realm, maintaining distance from troublesome humanity. Pharaohs exist because Ra needed human representatives to rule in his absence, bridging the gap between divine and mortal realms. And alcohol can transform consciousness because it transformed Sekhmet into Hathor, which meant intoxication had the power to change perception and personality.

Chapter 7: Tales and Wisdom

We've explored Egypt's great myths—the stories of gods, creation, death, and cosmic order. But Egyptian mythology wasn't just about divine drama in the heavens. It was also a living tradition of storytelling that taught lessons, explored moral questions, and entertained audiences for thousands of years.

The tales in this chapter are different from what we've covered so far. These aren't myths about how the world was created or how Osiris became king of the dead. Some of these tales come from what scholars call "wisdom literature"—texts that explored justice, fate, kindness, and the proper way to conduct yourself in the world. Others are folk tales and adventure stories that survived because they were too good to forget. The Egyptians didn't separate entertainment from moral instruction. A story could be thrilling and teach you something at the same time.

What's striking about these stories is how human they feel. Yes, gods sometimes appear in them, but the concerns are remarkably relatable. How do you get justice when someone more powerful wrongs you? What happens when you show kindness to a stranger? How do you survive when everything goes wrong? The answers the Egyptians gave to these questions tell us as much about their values as any temple inscription or religious text.

Let's hear some of these stories.

Isis and the Seven Scorpions

Isis walked alone through the marshes of the Nile Delta, her infant son Horus hidden in her arms. Set was hunting them. Everywhere she went, she had to hide. She could trust no one. The greatest goddess in Egypt was now a fugitive.

Seven scorpions accompanied her as bodyguards—Tefen, Befen, Mestet, Mestetef, Petet, Thetet, and Maatet. They walked in formation around her, three ahead, two on either side, and two behind. Their stings could kill anything that threatened the goddess.

As evening approached, Isis needed shelter. She came to a town in the marshes and approached the largest, finest house. A wealthy woman named Usert stood in the doorway. She saw Isis—dusty, tired, dressed in common clothes, and carrying a baby. She also saw the scorpions.

Usert slammed the door in Isis's face.

The scorpions bristled with rage. How dare this woman refuse shelter to their goddess? How dare she turn away a mother with a child?

But Isis said nothing. She turned away and continued walking.

At the edge of town, she found a poor woman's hut. The woman was a marsh girl, someone who gathered papyrus and caught fish to survive. Her home was barely more than reeds and mud. She owned almost nothing.

This woman—her name was Taha—saw Isis and the baby. She didn't ask questions. She didn't hesitate. "Come in," she said. "You and your child can rest here."

She gave Isis what little food she had. She offered her own sleeping mat. She brought water to wash the baby. She shared everything without expecting anything in return.

The scorpions waited outside and plotted their revenge.

Six of them pooled their venom, giving it all to the seventh: Tefen, the leader. Tefen crawled back through the town to Usert's fine house. He slipped under the door—scorpions can flatten themselves impossibly thin— and found Usert's young son sleeping in his bed.

Tefen stung him once, then left.

The boy woke up screaming. His body convulsed. Foam appeared at his mouth. His skin turned hot, then cold. He was dying.

Usert ran through the streets, pounding on doors, begging for help. "My son is dying! Please, someone help me! I'll pay anything! Please!"

But her neighbors remembered how she'd turned away the stranger with the baby. They remembered her pride, her wealth, and her sense that she was better than they were. They closed their doors, just as she had closed hers.

Usert heard her son's screams growing weaker. She ran through the streets with him in her arms, desperate, terrified, finding no help anywhere.

Isis heard the screaming. She came out of Taha's hut and saw Usert running with her dying child.

Isis could have walked away. Usert had refused her shelter. She had slammed a door in the face of a mother and child. Isis had every right to let justice take its course.

But Isis was a mother. And this was a child dying for his mother's mistake.

"Bring him here," Isis said.

Usert stumbled forward and collapsed at Isis's feet. "Please. Please save him. I'll give you anything. Please."

Isis took the boy and laid him on the ground. She placed her hands on his burning skin and spoke words of power. She called each scorpion by name. She called on them not as threats but as her companions, protectors, and friends.

"Tefen, withdraw your poison. Befen, take back your venom. Mestet, Mestetef, Petet, Thetet, Maatet, release this child. He has done nothing wrong. Let him live."

The venom retreated. The boy's convulsions stopped. Color returned to his face. He breathed normally and opened his eyes.

Usert wept and reached for her son, but Isis held him a moment longer.

"He will live," Isis said. "But remember this: Your wealth could not save him. Your fine house could not protect him. Only kindness saved him—the kindness I learned from Taha, who gave everything despite having nothing."

Then Isis returned the boy to his mother.

Usert understood. She took the poor marsh girl Taha into her household, gave her work, and treated her with respect. She never again turned away someone in need.

The scorpions learned something too. Revenge had nearly killed an innocent child. Justice wasn't the same as cruelty. Even the wronged must show mercy.

And Isis? She moved on with her son, still fleeing, still hiding. But she'd proven something important. Even when hunted, even when desperate, even when you have every reason to be hard, kindness still matters. Mercy still matters. Ma'at still matters.

The Eloquent Peasant

There was a peasant named Khun-Anup who lived in the Salt Field Oasis with his wife and children. He was poor but honest. He made his living by gathering salt and reeds.

One day, Khun-Anup loaded his donkeys with salt, reeds, skins, herbs, and everything else his family had produced. He was heading to the city to sell them and buy grain to feed his family through the coming months.

On the road, he had to pass through land owned by a man named Nemtynakht, who worked for the high steward Rensi. Nemtynakht saw Khun-Anup coming with his loaded donkeys and decided he wanted those goods for himself.

But he couldn't just rob the peasant openly. He needed an excuse.

Nemtynakht spread a cloth across the narrow part of the road. On one side was his barley field, and on the other side was a canal. The road was blocked. The peasant would have to either walk through the barley, which was illegal since it would damage crops, or through the canal, which was impossible with the loaded donkeys.

When Khun-Anup arrived at this spot, he stopped, confused.

"Please," he called to Nemtynakht. "Can you move your cloth? I need to pass."

"Walk around," Nemtynakht said.

"There is no around. There's your field or the water."

"That's not my problem."

Khun-Anup tried to navigate the narrow strip between the cloth and the field. His donkeys were careful, well-trained animals. But one of them, tempted by the barley, reached out and grabbed a single mouthful.

"Your donkey is eating my barley!" Nemtynakht shouted. "You've damaged my crops! I'm confiscating your donkeys and everything on them as payment!"

"It was one mouthful! I'll pay you for it!"

"Too late. These are mine now."

Nemtynakht's servants came out and seized the donkeys. They took everything—the salt, the reeds, the goods that represented months of Khun-Anup's family's labor. They beat the peasant and drove him away.

Khun-Anup was devastated. His family would starve without those goods. But he refused to accept this injustice.

He went to the high steward Rensi—Nemtynakht's superior—and demanded justice.

And here's where the story gets interesting.

Khun-Anup didn't just complain. He gave a speech about justice that was so eloquent, so perfectly expressed, so beautiful in its language that Rensi was stunned.

The high steward sent word to the pharaoh. "I have found a peasant who speaks like a scribe, who argues like a philosopher. His words are extraordinary."

The pharaoh sent back a message. "String him along. Don't give him justice yet. Let him keep talking. Write down everything he says."

So, Rensi refused to rule on Khun-Anup's case. He gave excuses, delays, and the bureaucratic runaround.

Khun-Anup kept coming back. He gave speech after speech, each one more eloquent than the last. Nine times he came before the high steward. Nine times he demanded justice. And each time, his words became more powerful, more poetic, and more devastating in their criticism of injustice.

He compared justice to the breath of life. He described Ma'at as a boat that could carry the oppressed to safety. He said that the high steward was like the rudder of the realm. If the rudder was crooked, the whole kingdom would veer off course.

He spoke about scales and balance. "You were appointed to be a balance, yet you lean to one side. You were made a dam to prevent floods, yet you let the water through to drown the weak."

His speeches were recorded word for word by scribes. They became famous, copied and recopied, and studied for their rhetoric and wisdom.

Finally, after the ninth speech, Rensi went to the pharaoh with all the transcripts.

The pharaoh read them and smiled. "This peasant understands justice better than most of my officials. Give him justice. Return his goods with compensation. And punish Nemtynakht. Give all his property to the peasant."

Rensi called Khun-Anup before him one last time.

"I have heard your words," he said. "Justice will be done."

He ordered Nemtynakht's entire estate seized and given to Khun-Anup. The peasant went from poor to wealthy in a single moment. More importantly, he'd proven that eloquence and truth were more powerful than corruption and theft.

But there's a twist to this story that scholars argue about.

Was Rensi testing Khun-Anup's persistence? Or was he just entertained by beautiful speeches while a peasant suffered? The text doesn't make this clear. Rensi delays justice nine times and lets Khun-Anup's family go hungry, all so the pharaoh can enjoy some good rhetoric.

The tale celebrates eloquence and justice, but it also shows the arbitrary nature of power. The peasant got justice only because his speeches entertained the powerful. If he'd been less eloquent, would he have gotten justice at all?

It's also a story about Ma'at being triumphant, although this story shows how fragile Ma'at could be, depending on the whims of those in power.

The eloquent peasant won. But how many peasants who weren't eloquent lost?

The Shipwrecked Sailor

An expedition had failed. Ships had been lost, men had died, and the survivor was returning to Egypt to face the pharaoh with terrible news. He sat on the boat, head in his hands, terrified of what would happen when he arrived.

His captain sat beside him. "You'll have to tell the pharaoh what happened. You're the only survivor."

"He'll kill me. The expedition failed. Ships sank. Everyone died but me."

"Then tell him a good story. Tell him the truth, but tell it well."

So, the sailor told his story to his captain, practicing what he'd say.

The story went like this:

"I was on a ship bound for the pharaoh's mines. We had 120 sailors, the best in Egypt. They'd seen the seas and the sky, and their hearts were braver than lions.

"But a storm rose. I've never seen waves so high. The wind was the breath of Set himself. The ship broke apart like a clay pot dropped on stone. Everyone died. Everyone except me.

"A wave threw me onto an island. I lay on the beach for three days, half-dead, alone.

"When I could finally move, I explored the island. It had everything—figs, grapes, onions, melons, fish, birds. I ate until I was full for the first time since the storm. I thanked the gods for saving me.

"Then I heard a sound like thunder. Trees shook. The ground trembled. I thought it was an earthquake.

"It wasn't an earthquake. It was a serpent.

"The serpent was enormous. It must have been thirty cubits long, covered in gold scales, with eyebrows of lapis lazuli. It moved toward me like a mountain sliding across the ground.

"'Who brought you to this island?' the serpent asked. Its voice shook my bones. 'Speak quickly, little man, or you'll be ash before you finish lying.'

"I threw myself flat on the ground. 'Great lord, I was on an expedition for the pharaoh. A storm destroyed our ship. Everyone died but me. A wave brought me here.'

"The serpent lowered its massive head and looked at me with eyes like pools of liquid gold. 'Do not be afraid, little man. Do not be afraid. The gods have let you live. Fate brought you to this island. You will stay here for four months. Then a ship will come and take you home. You will die in your own town, surrounded by family. That is your fate.'

"I thanked the serpent and asked, 'What is this place? Who are you?'

"The serpent told me its story. 'I lived here with my family—seventy-five serpents, all golden like me. My brothers, sisters, children, and one daughter I loved more than all the rest. We lived in peace.

"'Then a star fell from the sky. Fire came with it. The flames consumed everything. All seventy-five serpents burned. Only I survived because I was away hunting. I returned to find my family turned to ash.

"'So now I live alone on this island, waiting. Just as you wait to return home, I wait for death to reunite me with my family.'

"I felt sorry for this great creature, alone with its grief. 'When I return to Egypt,' I said, 'I'll tell the pharaoh about you. I'll send ships with incense and treasures as offerings. I'll make sure you're honored.'

"The serpent laughed, not cruelly but sadly. 'You have nothing I need, little man. I am the prince of Punt. This island is rich beyond Egypt's wealth. And when you leave, this island will vanish. You'll never find it again. It will disappear into the sea like foam.'

"Four months passed, exactly as the serpent predicted. A ship appeared on the horizon. I gathered gifts from the island—incense, spices, ivory, exotic animals—and prepared to leave.

"The serpent came to bid me farewell. 'Go safely home, little man. See your children again. Leave a good name in your town. That is my wish for you.'

"I thanked the serpent and boarded the ship. As we sailed away, I looked back. The island was gone. Nothing but open water remained, as if it had never existed.

"We sailed for two months and reached Egypt. I present these gifts to you, oh Pharaoh—treasures from an island that no longer existed, from a serpent who'd saved my life."

The captain listened to this entire tale and then said, "That's a good story. It is strange but good. The pharaoh might spare you if you tell it well."

This tale works on multiple levels. On the surface, it's an adventure story about a magical island. However, it's also about loss (the serpent's grief), about fate (the sailor's rescue), and about how stories can save us.

The sailor survived the storm by chance, but he might survive the pharaoh through storytelling. The serpent lost everything but lived on through the sailor's tale. The island vanished, but it exists forever in the story.

Sometimes survival isn't about strength or cunning. Sometimes it's about having a good story to tell.

The Tale of Two Brothers

There were two brothers who lived together and worked the same land. The older brother, Anubis (also named Anpu in texts), was married. The younger brother, Bata, was not. Bata lived in Anubis's household, helped with all the work, and was treated almost like a son.

Bata was extraordinary. He understood animals. When the cattle spoke to him about where the best grass grew, he listened and led them there. The harvests were always abundant when Bata worked the fields. He was stronger than any man in the region, and he worked harder than ten men combined.

Anubis loved his younger brother and relied on him completely.

One day, Anubis was away, and his wife was alone in the house with Bata. They'd been working in the fields, and Bata came back to get more seed.

Anubis's wife saw young, strong, handsome Bata. She approached him.

"Come," she said. "Let's spend an hour lying together. It will be good for you."

Bata was horrified. "What are you saying? You're like a mother to me! My brother is like a father! This is terrible, what you're suggesting. Never speak of this again. I won't tell anyone what you said. Just forget it happened."

He grabbed the seed and left, furious and disturbed.

But Anubis's wife panicked. If Bata told his brother what she'd done, she'd be disgraced, probably divorced, and possibly even killed. She had to act first.

When Anubis came home that evening, he found his wife lying on the floor, disheveled, with marks on her arms and face. She'd beaten herself to create false evidence.

"Your brother attacked me!" she cried. "When I was alone, he tried to force himself on me! I fought him off, and he ran away. If you don't kill him, I'll kill myself from shame!"

Anubis went cold with rage. His beloved younger brother had betrayed him in the worst possible way. He grabbed his spear and hid behind the barn door, waiting for Bata to return with the cattle.

The cattle came home at sunset, as always. But the lead cow stopped at the barn door and spoke to Bata (remember, Bata understood animals).

"Don't go in. Your brother is waiting behind the door with a spear. He means to kill you. Run!"

Bata looked and saw his brother's feet beneath the door. He ran.

Anubis chased him with the spear, determined to kill this traitor who'd violated his trust and attacked his wife.

Bata ran faster than he'd ever run, but Anubis was close behind, gaining ground.

Bata cried out to Ra. "My lord! You distinguish between truth and lies! You know what's right and what's wrong! Judge between us!"

Ra heard and created a river of crocodiles between the two brothers. Anubis stood on one bank. Bata stood on the other, panting, terrified.

"Why are you trying to kill me without even listening to my side?" Bata shouted across the water. "I never touched your wife! She propositioned me! I refused! She lied to you!"

Anubis hesitated. His brother's words rang with truth.

To prove his innocence, Bata did something extreme. He took a knife and castrated himself, throwing his severed flesh into the river where the crocodiles devoured it.

"There!" Bata cried. "If I'd wanted your wife, would I do this? I'm leaving. I'll go to the Valley of the Cedar. I'll cut out my heart and place it on the topmost flower of the cedar tree. If that tree is ever cut down, if my heart falls, come find me. I'll need your help. But until then, leave me alone. You chose to believe a lie instead of trusting your own brother."

Bata left, wounded and alone. Anubis went home and killed his wife. Then he mourned for his brother, knowing he'd made a terrible mistake.

Years passed. Bata lived alone in the Valley of the Cedar. The gods took pity on him and created a wife for him, a beautiful woman more lovely than any human woman.

But this wife, created by magic, was restless. One day, the sea tried to grab her as she walked along the shore. A lock of her hair came loose and floated away, all the way to Egypt, where it landed in the palace laundry. The hair smelled so wonderful that the pharaoh's clothes were perfumed by it.

The pharaoh wanted to know who this woman was. He sent soldiers to find her. They found Bata's wife in the Valley of the Cedar and brought her to Egypt. The pharaoh fell in love with her immediately and made her his queen.

The new queen feared Bata would come looking for her. She told the pharaoh, "There's a man in the Valley of the Cedar. Send men to cut down his cedar tree. He'll die, and then I'll truly be yours alone."

The pharaoh sent woodcutters, and they cut down the cedar. The flower holding Bata's heart fell, and Bata died.

Back in Egypt, Anubis felt something was wrong. He remembered his brother's words. So, he traveled to the Valley of the Cedar and found Bata's body. He searched for three years for the heart and finally found it.

Anubis placed the heart in water. It swelled and beat. He then placed it back in Bata's body.

Bata revived, but he transformed into a sacred bull. He went to Egypt, and when the pharaoh saw this marvelous bull, he declared it sacred and honored it.

But the bull spoke privately to the queen. "Look at me. I'm still alive."

She realized this was Bata. She went to the pharaoh and said, "I want to eat the liver of that bull."

"What? It's a sacred bull!"

"I want it anyway."

The pharaoh loved her too much to refuse. The bull was slaughtered. But as it died, two drops of blood fell by the palace gate. Overnight, two tall, beautiful *Persea* trees grew there.

The pharaoh honored these trees as sacred.

However, the trees spoke to the queen when she walked near them. "I'm still alive. You can't kill me."

She went to the pharaoh again. "I want these trees cut down. I want furniture made from them."

The pharaoh agreed. As the trees were being cut, a splinter flew into the queen's mouth. She swallowed it. And she became pregnant.

She gave birth to a son. The pharaoh loved this child and eventually made him crown prince.

When the old pharaoh died, the young man became pharaoh.

At his coronation, he revealed the truth. "I am Bata. I was a bull. I was trees. I am now your pharaoh. And you"—he pointed at the queen—"you tried to kill me three times. Justice will now be done."

The queen was executed. Bata sent for his brother Anubis. He forgave him completely and made him heir to the throne.

Bata ruled Egypt for thirty years. When he died, Anubis succeeded him and ruled wisely.

This tale is about false accusation, brotherly love tested to destruction, and the resilience of truth. No matter how many times Bata was killed, he returned. The innocent might suffer, but Ma'at would ultimately prevail.

It also might be the oldest recorded story of "Potiphar's wife." The false accusation motif shows up in biblical stories and many other traditions, but the Egyptians told it first.

Setne Khamwas and the Book of Thoth

Prince Setne Khamwas was the son of Pharaoh Ramesses II, but he cared less about ruling than about magic. He spent his days studying ancient texts, exploring tombs, and searching for lost knowledge. He was brilliant, ambitious, and convinced that if he could learn enough magic, he could rival the gods themselves.

One day, an old man approached him in a temple. "I know what you seek, Prince. You want power. I can tell you where to find the Book of Thoth. It was written by the god himself. It contains two spells. The first lets you understand every creature on earth. The second lets you see the gods themselves, even in their hidden forms."

Setne's heart raced. "Where is this book?"

"In a tomb at Saqqara. It's in a golden box, inside a silver box, inside a bronze box, inside an iron box, inside an ebony box, inside an ivory box. The tomb belongs to Naneferkaptah, who stole the book from Thoth's shrine at the bottom of the Nile. Thoth killed him for it. The book is guarded by serpents and scorpions. And Naneferkaptah's ghost still guards it."

"I'll get it," Setne said.

His brother Inaros tried to stop him. "This is madness. The book is cursed. Leave it alone."

But Setne wouldn't listen. He went to the tomb and descended into the burial chamber.

Inside, he saw three figures sitting as if they were alive: Naneferkaptah, his wife Ahwere, and their son Merib. They were ghosts, but they looked solid. And they were watching him.

"I've come for the Book of Thoth," Setne announced.

Ahwere spoke first, her voice sad and warning. "Don't take it. That book destroyed us. Let me tell you what happened.

"My husband Naneferkaptah was like you—brilliant and obsessed with magic. When he learned about the Book of Thoth, he had to have it. He took our son and me on a boat to where the book was hidden underwater. It was guarded by serpents.

"He used magic to part the waters and killed the serpents. He took the book. And the moment he touched it, Thoth knew.

"Thoth took our son first. Merib fell from the boat and drowned. My husband dove in with the book and used its magic to raise Merib's body, but our son was dead.

"We brought his body back to be buried. Then Thoth took me. I drowned too. My husband raised my body with the book's magic, but I was dead.

"He reached shore with two corpses. My husband buried us both in Memphis. And then Thoth took him. He drowned, still clutching the book.

"And now you want to take it? It will destroy you just as it destroyed us."

Setne listened but didn't care. "I'll take my chances. Give me the book."

Naneferkaptah's ghost stood. "Then you'll have to win it. Play me a game of senet. If you win, you can take it. If you lose, you leave and never return."

Setne agreed. They played.

Naneferkaptah won the first game. He used magic to drive Setne's body into the floor up to his knees.

They played again. Naneferkaptah won. Setne sank to his waist.

They played a third time. Naneferkaptah won again. Setne was buried to his neck in the tomb floor, unable to move.

Setne called out to his brother Inaros, who'd been waiting outside. Inaros came in with magic amulets and freed Setne from the floor.

Then Setne cheated. While Naneferkaptah was distracted, he grabbed the Book of Thoth and ran.

Behind him, the tomb went dark. He heard Ahwere weeping and Naneferkaptah shouting, "You'll bring it back! Everyone does!"

Setne didn't listen. He had the book. He'd won.

He read the first spell and suddenly understood every animal. Birds sang prophecies. Snakes whispered secrets. Fish told him about treasures beneath the Nile. The knowledge was intoxicating.

He read the second spell and saw the gods walking among humans, invisible to everyone else. He saw Ra's procession across the sky. He saw Thoth recording everything in his scrolls. He felt like he'd transcended human limitations.

But then the curse began.

He met a beautiful woman named Tabubu. She was unlike anyone he'd ever met. She was intelligent, alluring, and impossible to resist. She agreed to marry him but made strange demands.

"Kill your children," she said. "They're from your previous life. We should start fresh."

Under her spell, Setne did it. He had his own children killed.

"Sign over all your property to me," she demanded.

He did.

"Now make love to me here, in the street, in front of everyone. Prove you're not ashamed of me."

He started to comply, stripping off his clothes in public, completely under her power...

And then he woke up.

He was lying in the street, naked, surrounded by laughing crowds. The pharaoh was standing over him, disgusted. His children were alive. His property was still his. Tabubu had never existed.

It had all been an illusion sent by Thoth, showing Setne what he would lose if he kept the book.

Setne understood. He went back to the tomb at Saqqara.

Naneferkaptah's ghost was waiting. "I told you," he said quietly.

"I'm sorry," Setne said. He placed the Book of Thoth back in its golden box, inside the silver box, inside the bronze box, inside the iron box, inside the ebony box, inside the ivory box.

But Naneferkaptah shook his head. "This isn't enough. I want my wife and son returned to me. Bring Ahwere's and Merib's bodies from Memphis and bury them here with me. That's the price for stealing from the dead."

Setne did as asked. He brought the bodies of Ahwere and Merib from their tombs and reunited them with Naneferkaptah. The family was together again, even in death.

The tomb was sealed. The Book of Thoth was buried forever.

Setne left, humbled. He'd touched godly knowledge, and it had nearly destroyed him. Some books weren't meant to be read. Some magic was too dangerous to pursue. Some boundaries existed for good reasons.

The prince who wanted to rival the gods learned to respect limits instead.

Isis and Ra's Secret Name

Ra was old. The sun god had ruled for millennia, and his body showed it. He drooled. His hands trembled. Divine saliva dripped from his mouth as he walked the sky each day, and it fell to the earth below.

Isis watched. She was already the greatest magician among the gods, but Ra possessed something she didn't have—his secret name. In Egyptian magic, knowing someone's true name gave you power over them. Not their common name, not their titles, but the hidden name that contained their essence. Ra's secret name was the source of his ultimate power, and he'd never told anyone what it was.

Isis came up with an idea.

She waited until Ra passed overhead on his daily journey. She collected his saliva from the ground where it had fallen and mixed it with earth, creating clay. She shaped the clay carefully into a serpent, a creature that had never existed before.

Because it was formed from Ra's body, it was invisible to his power. His magic couldn't detect it, and his divine sight couldn't see it. She had created something that existed outside his knowledge and his control.

She placed the serpent on the path where Ra walked every day during his journey across the sky. When Ra passed by, the serpent struck. It bit him, injecting venom.

Ra screamed. The poison burned through his body like fire and ice simultaneously. He'd never felt pain like this.

"Help me!" Ra cried out. "Something has struck me! Something I don't recognize! My own hands didn't make it, none of you created it, yet it exists, and it's killing me!"

The other gods rushed to help, but no one could heal him. The venom was too powerful and too strange. Ra writhed in agony, his cries echoing across heaven and earth. The sun flickered. If Ra died, the world died with him.

Isis approached calmly. "Great Ra, what happened?"

"Something bit me," Ra gasped between waves of pain. "A serpent. But I didn't create it. I know everything I created, and this wasn't among them. How can something I didn't create harm me? The pain—it's burning through me, freezing me. I'm dying."

"I can heal you," Isis said quietly. "My magic is strong enough. But to cure you, I need to speak your true name. The spell won't work without it. I must invoke your secret name, the one you've never spoken aloud."

Ra hesitated even through his agony. His secret name was his power. It was the core of his being. If he revealed it, he'd be vulnerable. Someone who knew his true name could command him, control him, and unmake him if they wished.

But the pain was unbearable. He tried to bargain. "I am he who made heaven and earth. I am he who created the mountains and stretched out the great sea. I am he who made the hours and created the days. I am Khepri in the morning, Ra at noon, Atum in the evening..."

"Those are titles," Isis said gently but firmly. "Epithets. Descriptions. They're not your name. I need your true name. Your secret name. The one hidden in your heart that no one else knows."

The poison burned hotter. Ra's vision blurred. His body shook. He had no choice.

"Come closer," Ra whispered. "Let my name pass from my body directly to yours, where no one else can hear it. But swear you'll never speak it aloud. Swear you'll only pass it to your son Horus, and make him swear the same. This name must remain hidden."

Isis agreed. She leaned close.

Ra spoke his secret name. The ancient texts don't record what the name was. It was too sacred, too powerful to write down even in a myth. Some things are too dangerous to preserve.

Isis felt the power settle into her. Immediately, she spoke the healing spell. "Flow out, poison! Leave Ra's body! I, Isis, command you by his true name—the name I now possess. By his secret name, which gives me authority over all he created, depart, venom! Poison, dissolve! This I speak, and it is so!"

The poison obeyed. It couldn't resist a command spoken with Ra's true name backing it. Color returned to Ra's face. His trembling stopped. He was healed.

But he was changed. He'd given up his greatest secret, his ultimate power. The name that made him the supreme ruler of the gods now resided in Isis as well.

Isis had become the most powerful being in the universe. She possessed Ra's secret name, which meant she had authority over the sun god himself. If she wished, she could command him. But she kept her oath. She never spoke the name aloud, and she taught it only to Horus, binding him to the same secrecy.

Ra continued to rule, continued his daily journey across the sky. But the balance of power had shifted. The old god had been brought low by cleverness. The young goddess had gained supremacy through cunning rather than force.

The lesson is clear. Even the mightiest can be brought down by intelligence and planning. Even absolute power has vulnerabilities. And in Egyptian magic, names were everything—knowledge was power in its most literal, most dangerous form.

Isis never needed to use Ra's name against him. Possessing it was enough. The threat, unstated but understood, kept her position secure.

And she'd gotten it through a serpent, some clay, and patience.

The Prince and the Three Dooms

When the prince was born, the Seven Hathors came to prophesy his fate. These were aspects of the goddess Hathor who could see the future. They spoke of the destiny of every child.

They looked at the baby prince and said, "He will die by the crocodile, the serpent, or the dog."

The pharaoh was devastated. He'd waited years for a son, and now the gods had cursed him with this terrible fate. The pharaoh ordered a stone house built in the desert, far from any crocodiles, serpents, or dogs. The prince would live there, isolated, protected, and safe.

The boy grew up in that stone house with servants. He could see the desert through his window, but he could never walk in it. He had everything except freedom.

One day, he saw a man walking across the desert with a dog following him. "What's that animal?" he asked his servants.

"That's a dog, my prince."

"I want one."

The servants told the pharaoh. The pharaoh knew that dogs were one of the three fated deaths, but he couldn't bear to deny his son anything. He gave the prince a puppy.

The dog and the boy became inseparable. As the prince grew into a young man, he decided he'd had enough of his prison.

"I'm fated to die," he told his father. "Hiding won't change that. Let me go out into the world. Let me live before I die."

The pharaoh had no choice. He couldn't keep his son locked up forever. He gave the prince weapons, a chariot, supplies, and a warning. "Be careful. Watch for crocodiles, serpents, and dogs."

The prince left Egypt with his dog and traveled north to Syria. He heard that the prince of Naharin had a beautiful daughter who'd been locked in a tower. The tower had no doors and only one window high above the ground. The Syrian prince had declared, "Whoever can jump high enough to reach my daughter's window can marry her."

Princes from across the world tried. All failed.

The Egyptian prince arrived and saw the tower. He didn't tell anyone he was Egyptian royalty. He simply waited and watched.

When the other princes made their attempts and failed, the Egyptian prince stepped forward. He ran, jumped, and caught the windowsill. He pulled himself up and climbed into the tower.

The princess saw him and smiled. "Who are you?"

"A soldier's son from Egypt," he lied. "I've come to win you."

She loved him immediately. They talked all night. By morning, she'd decided that this was her husband, whether her father approved or not.

Her father was furious when he discovered that an Egyptian nobody had won his daughter. "I didn't build that tower for foreign soldiers!"

But the princess said, "If you send him away, I'll stop eating and drinking. I'll die of grief."

The Syrian prince loved his daughter. He had no choice. He accepted the Egyptian prince as his son-in-law.

At the wedding feast, the Egyptian prince told his new wife the truth. "I'm not just a soldier's son. I'm a prince of Egypt. And I'm cursed. The Seven Hathors prophesied I'll die by the crocodile, the serpent, or the dog."

His wife paled. "Then we'll be careful. We'll watch for these things."

They lived happily for a time. But one night, the prince drank too much wine and fell asleep in their chamber.

His wife saw a serpent emerge from a hole in the wall. It slithered toward her sleeping husband, ready to strike.

She didn't scream. She didn't run. She grabbed a bowl of wine and milk and set it before the serpent.

The serpent drank. It got drunk and became sluggish and confused. She grabbed an ax and killed it.

When her husband woke, she showed him the dead serpent. "This was your death. But I killed it."

One doom was defeated.

They traveled back toward Egypt. They had to cross a river where a crocodile lived. The crocodile had been in a magical stalemate for months with a water demon. Each dawn, they fought. Each sunset, they separated, neither able to kill the other.

When the prince swam across the river, the crocodile caught him.

"I should eat you," the crocodile said. "But I'll make you an offer. Help me kill the water demon, and I'll let you live."

"How can I help? I'm human."

"The demon is bound by magic during daylight. If you kill it then, I'll be free, and I'll spare you."

The prince and the crocodile made some kind of bargain. The prince might have agreed to help kill the demon in exchange for his life.

We don't know for sure because the papyrus breaks off completely.

We don't know what happened next. Did the prince defeat the crocodile doom? Was he killed? What about the dog, his faithful companion since childhood? Did the third doom ever come for him? Did his wife save him again?

The Egyptians who wrote this story knew the ending. But time has taken it from us. The papyrus is too damaged to read further. We're left with a prince who defeated the serpent and faced the crocodile, but his final fate remains unknown.

Maybe that's fitting for a story about destiny. We can see fate approaching, we can struggle against it, we can even defeat parts of it, but we never really know how our own story ends until it's over. The prince's tale is unfinished. In a way, everyone's is.

Chapter 8: Mythology in Action

The myths we've discussed weren't just stories Egyptians told around fires or read in books. They shaped Egyptian civilization at every level. Every pyramid, every temple, every festival, every pharaoh was legitimized and structured by these myths. The stories provided the framework that made Egyptian society function as it did.

The Pharaoh as a God: Living as the "Living Horus"

The pharaoh wasn't just a king. He was treated as a god in Egyptian ideology and ritual. The official theology presented him as the living embodiment of Horus and the son of Ra, even though everyone could see he was born human, aged, and died like any mortal.

This concept seems strange to modern people. We're used to separation between church and state and between religious and political authority. However, Egypt had no such division. The pharaoh was both king and god. He maintained cosmic order. He kept the sun rising, the Nile flooding, and chaos at bay.

Remember from Chapter 3 how Horus won the throne of Egypt after defeating Set? Throughout most of Egyptian history, the reigning pharaoh was identified with Horus, ruling Egypt as Horus had ruled it after reclaiming his father's throne. When a pharaoh died, he became Osiris (joining the dead god in the afterlife), and the new pharaoh became Horus.

The pharaoh was also the son of Ra. The sun god was his father. This parentage gave him authority over Egypt and cosmic significance. As Ra's son, the pharaoh represented order on earth. He connected the human and godly realms.

The pharaoh's power was absolute in theory. In principle, he owned all the land in Egypt, though in practice, land was controlled by temples, officials, and private individuals. He commanded all military forces. He appointed all officials and made all the laws. His word was treated as a decree from the gods. No constitution limited him. No parliament checked him. No court could overrule him.

Being a god-king didn't mean the pharaoh personally controlled every detail; it just meant he was cosmically responsible for everything.

The royal titulary proved this godhood through five names given at coronation. Each name emphasized a different aspect of kingship. Think of them as the pharaoh's credentials—proof he was qualified to rule as a god.

The Horus name identified the king as the living Horus. This was the oldest royal title, going back to the very beginning of Egyptian kingship. It was written inside a serekh, a rectangular frame representing the palace façade topped by a falcon (Horus).

The Two Ladies name invoked Nekhbet (vulture goddess of Upper Egypt) and Wadjet (cobra goddess of Lower Egypt). This emphasized the king's rule over the unified land.

The Golden Horus name was more mysterious. Scholars debate its exact meaning, but it seems to be related to the king's eternal, imperishable nature, like gold, which doesn't tarnish or decay.

The serekh of Pharaoh Djoser.[25]

The prenomen (throne name) was the king's official regnal name, usually incorporating Ra's name. You'd see this in most inscriptions. It was written in a cartouche, an oval rope loop symbolizing the king's rule over everything the sun encircles.

Examples of cartouches.[26]

The nomen (birth name) was the king's personal name, and it was also written in a cartouche. This was the name given at birth before he became king.

The Sed festival renewed the king's power after thirty years of rule. This was a jubilee celebration, but it came with cosmic stakes. The pharaoh had to prove he was still capable of maintaining Ma'at, still strong enough to rule, and still worthy of divine kingship.

The festival involved elaborate ceremonies spread over several days. The king performed ritual runs between boundary markers to show he could still traverse his kingdom's boundaries. He was symbolically crowned again as king of Upper and Lower Egypt in separate ceremonies, wearing the White Crown of Upper Egypt and the Red Crown of Lower Egypt. He received the homage of the gods' statues carried in procession from temples across Egypt. Offerings were made to all the gods. Rituals were performed reenacting the king's coronation and divine birth. The king's divine power was magically renewed through these performances.

Historical records show some pharaohs celebrated multiple Sed festivals. Ramesses II celebrated his first Sed festival in his thirtieth year and then held thirteen more over his long reign. Amenhotep III celebrated at least three. These were expensive, elaborate affairs requiring massive resources and the participation of priests from throughout Egypt.

Why was this renewal necessary? Well, Egyptian kingship depended on the king's ability to function. A weak king couldn't maintain Ma'at. An incompetent king let chaos creep in. The Sed festival proved the king was still fit to rule. If he was too old or weak to perform the ceremonies—if he couldn't complete the ritual runs or couldn't stand through the long ceremonies—that suggested maybe it was time for a new pharaoh.

Some scholars speculate that in early periods, the Sed festival might have originated in ritual renewal traditions involving symbolic or actual sacrifice of an aging king, though direct evidence for this practice is lacking. By historical times, any such tradition (if it ever existed) had been replaced by ritual renewal through ceremony rather than violence.

This brings up an uncomfortable reality. If the pharaoh was supposed to maintain Ma'at and things went badly—for instance, if there was drought, famine, a military defeat, or plague—that suggested the king was failing his responsibility. Failed pharaohs could be overthrown, assassinated, or forced to abdicate. Being a god-king didn't mean absolute security. It meant absolute responsibility.

We know from historical records that several pharaohs were murdered or overthrown. Amenemhat I was probably assassinated in his bedroom despite being a successful and capable ruler. The Harem Conspiracy during the reign of Ramesses III involved palace officials and royal wives attempting to murder the pharaoh through both physical violence and magical attacks. Pharaoh Teti was murdered by his bodyguards.

The First Intermediate Period (roughly 2181–2055 BCE) showed what happened when pharaohs failed repeatedly. Multiple rulers claimed to be the pharaoh at the same time. The system fractured. Local governors effectively became independent, and Egypt fragmented politically. This wasn't supposed to be possible if the pharaoh was truly a god, but it happened anyway. Eventually, a new strong king (Mentuhotep II) reunified Egypt and restored traditional kingship.

Royal women held important religious roles too. The God's Wife of Amun was a high priestess position, and it was especially powerful during the later New Kingdom and Third Intermediate Period. This woman— usually the king's daughter or wife—performed rituals for Amun and wielded considerable political and economic power. She was married to the god, not to a human husband. She couldn't have children, or at least was expected not to. When she died or retired, she adopted a successor, usually a royal princess, ensuring the position continued.

The God's Wife controlled enormous resources. She owned land, collected taxes, commanded staff, and managed temple finances. Some of the God's Wives wielded power rivaling or exceeding that of the pharaoh in religious matters. Inscriptions show them making offerings to gods, leading processions, and performing rituals usually reserved for the king. They wore the uraeus (royal cobra) on their foreheads, a symbol of kingship reserved for pharaohs.

Queens were associated with goddesses, particularly Hathor and Isis. The queen was the mother who would bear the next Horus, continuing the cycle of god-kingship. She participated in rituals alongside the king, appeared in religious art wearing crowns and carrying symbols of power, and had her own role in maintaining order.

Some queens exercised tremendous power. Hatshepsut began as regent for her young stepson Thutmose III but eventually declared herself pharaoh, ruling as a king (complete with false beard and male royal regalia) for about twenty years. Nefertiti apparently wielded extraordinary influence during her husband's reign. Tiye, wife of Amenhotep III, corresponded with foreign rulers and advised her son, Akhenaten, who later attempted a religious revolution. Nefertari, wife of Ramesses II, was honored with her own magnificent temple at Abu Simbel, standing as an equal to her husband.

Royal mothers held a special status as well. The king's mother had given birth to a living god. She was the mother of Horus, having conceived through supernatural intervention, according to the myths. Temple reliefs depicted gods impregnating queens to produce godly pharaohs. These weren't meant literally—everyone knew the biological facts—but they expressed the theological truth that pharaohs were gods, not merely men.

Now for the awkward truth: god-kingship was partly fiction. Everyone knew the king was born human. They saw him eat, sleep, age, and die like any human. The myths said he was a god, but reality was more complicated.

Egyptians handled this through what scholars call "dual consciousness," meaning they maintained two truths simultaneously. Yes, the king was human, but he was also a god. Both were true at the same time in different contexts. In religious rituals, he was fully godly. In daily administration, he was a skilled ruler. In propaganda, he was perfect. In reality, he had flaws.

The system worked because everyone participated in the fiction. The myths said the pharaoh was a god, so treating him as such made the myths real. And if the myths were real, Ma'at was maintained, the Nile would flood, and Egypt would prosper. The fiction had practical value.

This practical aspect kept pharaohs accountable in a strange way. They had to succeed, not just politically but also cosmically. Military victories, successful Nile floods, completed building projects, and diplomatic achievements all proved the king was maintaining Ma'at. Failures suggested problems with the cosmic order itself.

One pharaoh tested these limits dramatically. Akhenaten ruled in the 14th century BCE and decided to overthrow the entire religious system. He attempted to replace all of Egypt's gods with a single deity, the Aten, the sun disk itself.

This wasn't a minor reform. Akhenaten closed temples throughout Egypt and ordered Amun's name chiseled off monuments and temple walls. He stopped funding the priesthoods. He even built a new capital city in the desert, Akhetaten (modern Amarna), dedicated entirely to the worship of the Aten. He declared himself and his wife Nefertiti the sole intermediaries between humanity and the divine.

The pharaoh was supposed to maintain Ma'at and keep the gods happy. Akhenaten was doing the opposite by actively destroying temples, firing priests, and erasing divine names. He was using his authority as a god-king to unmake the cosmic order his predecessors had maintained for nearly two thousand years.

The experiment lasted about seventeen years. When Akhenaten died, the backlash was swift. His young successor, probably his son, the famous Tutankhamun, reversed everything. The temples reopened, and priests returned. Amun's name was restored. The capital moved back to Thebes. It was as if Akhenaten's revolution had never happened.

But the pharaohs went further. Later kings erased Akhenaten's name from official records and destroyed his monuments. In official king lists, the years of his reign were skipped or attributed to other rulers.

The Akhenaten episode reveals something important about the pharaoh's power. The pharaoh theoretically had absolute authority, but that authority depended on maintaining the traditional order, not destroying it. A pharaoh who violated Ma'at—even in the name of religious reform—was not a legitimate pharaoh. The system could reject a god-king who failed to act like one.

The Temples: Keeping the Gods Fed and Happy So the World Doesn't End

Temples weren't churches where people worshiped. They were houses for gods—literal residences where deities lived in statue form. The temple was the god's palace, and priests were their servants. Their job was to take care of the deity so the deity would take care of Egypt.

Every day, priests performed the same rituals. These weren't optional ceremonies; they were seen as essential for maintaining order.

The daily ritual began before dawn. Priests entered the temple in the pre-dawn darkness, carrying lamps and torches. They purified themselves in the sacred lake, washing away any impurities that might offend the deity.

The high priest (or the pharaoh, when he was present) approached the sanctuary, the innermost room of the temple where the statue lived in a shrine. He broke the clay seal on the shrine's doors. This seal had been placed the night before. Breaking it woke the deity.

The doors opened. The statue sat inside, exactly where it had been placed last night. The priest greeted it with hymns and prayers.

Then came the morning ablutions. The priests washed the statue, anointed it with sacred oils, applied cosmetics, dressed it in fresh, clean linen, and adorned it with jewelry. They actually washed, dressed, and decorated the statue just like you'd attend to an important person.

Why would they do this? Because Egyptians believed the deity's ka lived in the statue. The statue wasn't just a representation. Egyptians treated it as the god's body on earth. During its consecration, priests performed the Opening of the Mouth ceremony (you might remember that from the afterlife section). That's what made the statue spiritually alive. And once it was alive, it needed care.

After dressing the deity, the priests presented offerings. They gave the deity food, drink, incense, and flowers—the finest Egypt could provide. Bread, beer, meat, fruits, vegetables, wine, and honey were all laid before the statue.

The deity didn't physically eat the food. It consumed the ka (spiritual essence) of the offerings. Once that spiritual essence had been consumed, the physical food was removed and distributed to the priests as payment for their service.

More hymns, more prayers, and more rituals followed. Incense was burned. Sacred texts were recited. Then the priest backed out of the sanctuary, sweeping away his footprints with a broom so no trace of human presence remained. The doors closed. The clay seal was applied. The deity rested until the next ritual.

This happened daily in major temples across Egypt, though practices varied by region. The gods in important cult centers were attended to constantly.

Only priests could enter the sanctuary. In most periods, only they saw the statues housed in the innermost chambers. The innermost parts of temples were restricted. You had to be ritually pure, properly initiated, and authorized to enter. Most Egyptians never went past the temple's outer courts.

This restriction was enforced strictly. Temple walls had inscriptions warning unauthorized people to stay out. The areas beyond the outer courtyard were sacred space where only the purified could safely tread. Violating these boundaries was a serious offense.

The outer courts were where ordinary people interacted with the temple. You could enter the outer courtyard, make offerings at subsidiary altars, consult priests about legal or medical problems, seek oracles, and participate in public ceremonies. But you couldn't go deeper into the temple. You had to trust that the priests were doing their job.

Temples owned massive amounts of land. They weren't just religious institutions; they were also economic powerhouses. Temple lands were worked by farmers who gave a portion of their produce to the temple. Those offerings fed the god (spiritually), fed the priests (physically), and supported the temple's operations.

The Temple of Amun at Karnak eventually became the largest religious complex ever built. It was a vast city of temples, chapels, obelisks, and statues covering over two hundred acres. It employed thousands of people. At its height, the temple owned hundreds of thousands of acres of agricultural land, controlled shipping and trade, and wielded enormous political influence.

Temples also received donations from the pharaoh, tribute from conquered territories, and gifts from wealthy individuals seeking divine favor. Major temples controlled enormous wealth and employed thousands of people, including priests, administrators, farmers, craftsmen, guards, musicians, dancers, and more. Temple workshops produced bread, beer, linen, pottery, metalwork, and other goods. Temple granaries stored surplus grain. Temple treasuries held gold, silver, and precious stones.

The priesthood itself was hierarchical and specialized. The high priest (called "First Prophet" in Egyptian) managed the temple and performed the most sacred rituals. Below him were priests with different responsibilities. Lector priests recited spells, wab priests performed purification rituals, and sem priests handled funerary rites. Some priesthoods were hereditary. Others were appointed by the pharaoh. Many priests served part-time, rotating in for one month out of every four and pursuing other professions the rest of the year.

Women could serve as priestesses, particularly in the cults of female deities like Hathor. Female musicians and singers performed in temple rituals. The God's Wife of Amun, which we talked about earlier, was the highest-ranking religious position a woman could hold, wielding power comparable to the high priest of Amun.

The temple was creation itself in miniature form. The architecture was the cosmos. The floor was the earth. The ceiling was painted with stars, representing the sky itself. Columns were shaped like papyrus or lotus plants—the primeval marsh where creation began. The sanctuary, the holy of holies, was the primeval mound where Atum first stood at creation.

The pylon gateway at the temple's entrance was the horizon, or the *akhet*, where the sun rose. Passing through the pylon meant entering a sacred realm. Each courtyard brought you deeper into that realm and closer to the moment of creation.

Festivals and Funerals: How Ordinary People Celebrated the Myths

Festivals gave ordinary Egyptians access to their gods. These were huge public celebrations when statues came out of their sanctuaries, traveled through the streets, visited other temples, and allowed the common people to witness their godly presence.

The Opet Festival

The Opet festival was the biggest, most spectacular public event in Thebes. Held annually during the second month of the flood season (roughly July to August), it celebrated the connection between the pharaoh and the god Amun-Ra. The festival lasted anywhere from eleven days to nearly a month, depending on the period.

The festival's centerpiece was a grand procession. Priests carried Amun's sacred statue from Karnak Temple south along the Nile to Luxor Temple, about two miles away. The statue remained hidden inside an elaborate shrine mounted on a sacred boat, a barque. This wasn't a real boat; it was a ceremonial vessel carried on poles by dozens of priests.

Massive crowds lined the route. This was one of the few times ordinary people could witness the procession of the god's shrine, though the statue itself remained hidden inside. The golden shrine glittered in the sun. Priests in white linen carried it carefully, chanting hymns. Musicians played sistrums (sacred rattles), drums, and harps. Singers performed sacred songs. The air was filled with incense smoke.

The procession included other gods too. Mut (Amun's wife) and Khonsu (their son) traveled in their own sacred boats. High officials, priests, and the pharaoh himself participated. The pharaoh walked alongside or in front of Amun's boat, demonstrating his special relationship with the god.

People brought offerings like food, flowers, and small statues. The procession sometimes went by land and sometimes by water. In land processions, the boats were carried through streets packed with spectators. In water processions, the sacred boats were placed on real ships and sailed down the Nile, accompanied by smaller boats filled with celebrants.

When the procession reached Luxor Temple, the statues entered the sanctuary for private rituals. The pharaoh and high priests performed secret ceremonies inside. These were known as "mysteries," and ordinary people weren't allowed to witness or know about them. These rituals reaffirmed the pharaoh's divine kingship and renewed his connection to Amun.

After the rituals concluded at Luxor, the gods returned to Karnak in another grand procession. The festival ended with final offerings and ceremonies. The statues returned to their dark sanctuaries, and the crowds dispersed. Thebes returned to normal—until next year.

The Opet festival reinforced everything that held Egyptian society together. It demonstrated the pharaoh's divine authority and gave ordinary people a rare opportunity to witness the divine through a public procession. It essentially created community through shared celebration.

The Khoiak Festival

The Khoiak festival was completely different. It was quieter and more solemn, focused on death and rebirth. It commemorated Osiris's death and resurrection, falling during the fourth month of the flood season (roughly October to November).

Remember Osiris's story from Chapter 3? Set murdered him, dismembered his body, and scattered the pieces. Isis gathered the fragments and, with magic, brought him back to life, not to rule the living but to become the king of the dead. The Khoiak festival reenacted this cycle of death and resurrection.

The festival's central ritual involved creating "Osiris beds," molds shaped like Osiris filled with soil and planted with grain seeds. These molds were typically mummiform (shaped like mummies) with Osiris's distinctive features. Priests filled them with Nile mud and silt, planted barley or emmer wheat, and then watered them carefully.

The grain grew. Green shoots emerged from the "body" of Osiris. The god was reborn through vegetation. Death produced life.

Osiris didn't just represent grain; he *was* grain. His body, dismembered and scattered, became the fields of Egypt. His resurrection was the harvest.

The festival connected Osiris's myth to agricultural reality. Egypt's life depended on the Nile flood bringing fertile silt. That silt grew grain. Without death (the flood destroying old growth), there could be no life (the new harvest). Osiris embodied this cycle.

The timing wasn't accidental. The festival fell just after the Nile flood receded, when fields were ready for planting. The agricultural calendar and religious calendar aligned. Farmers planting their fields participated in the god's rebirth. Every seed planted was Osiris returning to life.

The festival lasted several weeks, with different rituals on different days. Some were public, while others were private. The emotional journey moved from mourning to celebration, matching Osiris's story, which goes from grief at his murder, to hope during the search, to joy at his restoration.

For ordinary Egyptians, the Khoiak festival offered hope. Yes, death was real, but Osiris proved death wasn't the end. Every year, he died. And every year, he returned. The grain proved it.

Death and Burial for Ordinary Egyptians

We have discussed elaborate mummification, expensive tombs, and fancy grave goods, but that was for the wealthy elite. What about everyone else? What about the farmers, craftsmen, servants, and laborers who made up the vast majority of Egypt's population?

Poor and middle-class Egyptians still tried to provide proper burials. They couldn't afford proper mummification or rooms full of grave goods, but they did what they could. Death rites mattered to everyone, not just the rich.

The poorest Egyptians received simple burials. The body might be wrapped in reed mats or cheap linen, then placed in a simple pit grave or a reused tomb. There were minimal grave goods. There would be no coffin or elaborate tomb.

However, even these simple burials followed patterns established by elite practices. The body was positioned carefully, facing west toward the realm of the dead. Basic offerings were left, such as bread, beer, and simple foods. There could be a few pottery vessels, worn-out tools, or personal possessions. The intent was the same as elite burials: provide the deceased with supplies for the afterlife.

Natural mummification sometimes occurred accidentally. Egypt's hot, dry climate and sandy soil could naturally desiccate bodies, preserving them without artificial mummification. Bodies buried in simple pit graves in the desert sand often survived better than expensively mummified bodies in elaborate tombs where moisture and insects could get in. The poor sometimes achieved better preservation by accident than the rich did by intention.

Middle-class Egyptians, like successful craftsmen, scribes, minor officials, and prosperous farmers, could afford more. They paid for basic mummification, which included removing organs, drying the body with natron, and wrapping the body in linen. This was not the extensive seventy-day process with the finest materials that elites received, but it was enough to preserve the body. They purchased simple wooden coffins, often reused or mass-produced. They rented space in communal tombs or built small mud-brick tomb chapels. Some could afford abbreviated Book of the Dead spells. These were cheaper versions with less decoration.

Shabtis depended on one's wealth, from hundreds for the rich to one or none for the poor.

Family obligations were the same regardless of wealth. Living relatives had to maintain the deceased's tomb, leave offerings, speak the deceased's name, and perform rituals. For the poor, this might mean visiting a simple grave annually with bread and beer. For the rich, it meant maintaining elaborate tomb chapels with daily offerings.

Failure to provide proper burial was catastrophic. A body left unburied, exposed to scavengers or destroyed by the elements, meant that the person had no chance at the afterlife. The worst punishment, worse than execution, was to be denied burial. Criminals guilty of terrible crimes might have their bodies thrown into the Nile or left in the desert. This destroyed them permanently, preventing any existence in the afterlife.

This means even the poorest families scraped together resources for burial. They might go into debt for it. A proper burial was worth any sacrifice because the alternative—eternal death, permanent obliteration— was unthinkable.

The End of the Gods: How Christianity and Islam Eventually Replaced the Old Ways

The Egyptian religion lasted over three thousand years. That's longer than Christianity has existed. Longer than Islam. Longer than most civilizations have lasted. But nothing lasts forever.

The end came gradually. No single moment killed the Egyptian religion. It eroded over centuries, weakened by foreign conquest, economic pressure, religious competition, and cultural change.

Christianity arrived in Egypt during the 1ˢᵗ century CE. According to tradition, Saint Mark founded the Egyptian church in Alexandria around 42 CE. Early Egyptian Christianity (also called Coptic Christianity) grew slowly at first, spreading among urban populations and among educated Greeks.

For the first few centuries, Egyptian traditional religion and Christianity coexisted. Some Egyptians converted to Christianity. Others maintained the old gods. Many probably hedged their bets, participating in both religious systems. The temples continued functioning, and priests still performed daily rituals. The pharaohs were gone (Egypt became a Roman province), but the gods remained.

The coexistence wasn't always peaceful. Christian monks vandalized pagan temples, defacing images of gods and destroying "idols." Traditional priests resisted Christian expansion. Religious violence occurred sporadically. However, for several centuries, both religions operated at the same time in Egypt.

Early Egyptian Christianity developed its own character. It emphasized asceticism—monks withdrawing to the desert for prayer and contemplation. The Egyptian desert that had once been Set's domain became filled with Christian hermits and monasteries. Some scholars see parallels between the hermit monks and the ancient tradition of priests spending time in desert purification.

Coptic Christianity also maintained connections to ancient Egyptian culture. The Coptic calendar was based on the ancient Egyptian calendar. Some Coptic festivals fell on dates that had been sacred to ancient gods. The Virgin Mary shared some attributes with Isis. For instance, both were divine mothers and protectors. Coptic (the final form of the ancient Egyptian language) survived as a liturgical language in the Coptic Church, though it's no longer spoken daily.

The turning point came in the 4th century CE when the Roman Empire officially embraced Christianity. Emperor Theodosius I issued edicts in the 390s CE ordering the closure of pagan temples throughout the empire. Egypt was included.

Temple closures happened gradually. Some temples were destroyed. Zealous Christians smashed statues, defaced relief carvings, and demolished sacred structures. Others were converted into churches, the sacred architecture repurposed for new gods. Christian crosses were carved over ancient hieroglyphs. Church altars were built in former sanctuaries where the Egyptian gods' statues once resided.

Some temples continued operating in a reduced capacity, especially in remote areas where imperial authority was weak and traditional religion remained strong. The Temple of Isis at Philae, located on an island in the Nile south of Aswan, remained the last functioning Egyptian temple. Despite the official closure edicts of the 390s, Philae continued operating for another 150 years, finally closing in the mid-6th century CE (around

537 to 550 CE). The temple's remote location and the strength of Isis worship in the region allowed it to survive longer than any other temple.

The last datable hieroglyphic inscription was carved at Philae Temple in 394 CE. It is a simple text, recording a date and an offering. Nothing dramatic—just the last time someone carved sacred writing in the ancient script. The skill of reading and writing hieroglyphs died out within a generation or two. Priests who knew the ancient texts grew old and died without training successors.

By the 5th century, no one could read hieroglyphs anymore. The texts carved on temple walls, written on papyri, and inscribed on tombs became mysterious symbols. The words of the gods fell silent, unreadable and forgotten.

This was a catastrophic cultural loss. Imagine if everyone suddenly forgot how to read English, Spanish, or Chinese. Books would become decoration. All knowledge preserved only in writing became inaccessible. That's what happened to the Egyptian religion.

The Islamic conquest in the 7th century CE completed the transformation. Arab armies conquered Egypt in 642 CE, bringing Islam to a country that was predominantly Christian. Over the following centuries, most Egyptians converted to Islam. Arabic replaced Coptic as the daily language, and Islamic culture became dominant.

Folk practices probably absorbed some elements that echoed the ancient religion. Protective charms and agricultural rituals tied to the Nile had patterns with ancient roots, though people no longer remembered why. The veneration of saints resembled the old worship of gods in some ways. But these were fragments and echoes, not a conscious continuation of the old religion.

The last priests of Isis at Philae probably did not realize they were the final practitioners of a religion that had existed for three thousand years. They just performed their rituals, made their offerings, and eventually died without successors.

For over a thousand years, the gods were silent. It was not until Jean-François Champollion deciphered hieroglyphs in 1822 that the voices of ancient Egypt could be heard again.

Conclusion

You can see Egyptian influence everywhere once you know what to look for. The Washington Monument is an obelisk. Hollywood keeps making movies about mummies and pharaohs. Museums use pyramid shapes to suggest permanence and ancient wisdom. The concept of moral judgment after death—your deeds being weighed, your fate determined by how you lived—appears in multiple religious traditions that came after the Egyptian religion. Whether these later traditions directly borrowed from Egypt or independently developed similar ideas, the parallels reflect human concerns about justice and what happens after we die.

However, the real legacy of Egyptian mythology isn't in architecture or movies. It's in the ideas.

What These Myths Teach Us

Strip away the animal-headed gods and elaborate rituals, and Egyptian mythology still has things to say.

Order takes work. The Egyptians knew that civilization doesn't run itself. The sun had to be defended every night. The rituals had to be performed every morning. Society had to be governed justly. Nothing stayed good automatically. That's still true. Democracy doesn't maintain itself. Justice doesn't happen without effort. The things we value fall apart if we don't actively protect them.

Death isn't the end of the story. The Egyptians weren't morbid; they were hopeful. They believed consciousness continued after death, that you could prepare for what came next, and that you'd see your loved ones again. Whether you believe in an afterlife or not, their approach suggests something worth considering: what we do matters beyond our own lifetime. We can influence what survives us.

Power comes with responsibility. The pharaoh wasn't just powerful. He was also responsible for keeping the universe running properly. If he failed, he could be overthrown. His authority came with obligations. The Egyptians understood that leaders aren't just privileged; they owe something to the people they rule.

Balance beats winning. Ma'at wasn't about crushing chaos forever. That was impossible. It was about maintaining balance. There shouldn't be too much order (which becomes stagnation), and there shouldn't be too much chaos (which becomes destruction). There had to be just enough of each, adjusted constantly. Absolute order is tyranny. Total chaos leads to collapse. The sweet spot is in between.

Stories matter. The Egyptians understood that the myths a society tells determine how that society works. Tell stories about god-kings maintaining cosmic order, and you get one kind of civilization. Tell different stories, and you get different results. Myths aren't just entertainment; they're instructions for how to live.

The Egyptian myths lasted three thousand years because they worked. They gave people meaning, structure, hope, and purpose. They explained the world in ways that made sense.

When Christianity and Islam eventually replaced the Egyptian religion, they filled the same needs. They had different answers to the same human questions.

We study Egyptian mythology today not because we believe it literally but because it shows us something about how humans make sense of being alive. Every culture needs stories that explain where we came from, why we're here, what happens when we die, and how we should live.

The gods fell silent when the last temple closed. But the questions they answered—and the ways they answered them—haven't disappeared.

Glossary of Names: A "Who's Who" Cheat Sheet

Major Gods

Amun — "The Hidden One." King of the gods during much of the New Kingdom. Originally a local deity of Thebes who rose to supreme power. Often combined with Ra as Amun-Ra. Typically depicted as a man with a tall plumed crown.

Anubis — Jackal-headed god associated with mummification and guiding the dead. Protected tombs and guided souls through the afterlife. In various traditions, son of Osiris (or sometimes Set) and Nephthys.

Atum — "The Complete One." The creator god in Heliopolitan theology who emerged from Nu and began creation. Associated with the setting sun. One of the forms of Ra.

Bastet — Cat goddess. Originally a fierce lioness deity, later became a gentler cat associated with protection, joy, music, and dance. Daughter of Ra.

Bes — Dwarf god with a grotesque face and lion features. Protected homes, children, childbirth, and families. Not depicted in profile like other gods but face-forward.

Geb — Earth god. Depicted as a man lying beneath the sky goddess Nut. Father of Osiris, Isis, Set, and Nephthys. His laughter caused earthquakes.

Hathor — Cow goddess (or woman with cow horns). Goddess associated with love, beauty, joy, music, dance, motherhood, and fertility. Could also manifest as fierce (as Sekhmet). Often connected with the Eye of Ra.

Horus — Falcon-headed god. Son of Osiris and Isis in the Osirian tradition. God of the sky and kingship. The reigning pharaoh was typically identified as the living Horus. His eyes were associated with the sun and moon. Won the throne from Set after an 80-year contest.

Isis — The great goddess. Wife of Osiris, mother of Horus. Goddess associated with magic, healing, protection, and motherhood. Known in many texts for her intelligence and magical power, including learning Ra's secret name.

Khnum — Ram-headed god. Potter who shaped humans on his wheel and controlled the Nile's flood. Guardian of the Nile's source.

Ma'at — Goddess of truth, justice, order, balance, and harmony. Depicted with an ostrich feather on her head. This feather was used to weigh hearts in judgment. Ma'at was both a goddess and the fundamental principle of cosmic order.

Nephthys — Sister of Isis and Osiris. Wife of Set but sided with Isis during the Osiris crisis. Goddess of mourning, night, and childbirth. Helped protect the dead.

Nut — Sky goddess. Depicted as a woman arching over the earth (Geb). Swallowed the sun each evening and gave birth to it each morning. Mother of Osiris, Isis, Set, Nephthys, and sometimes Horus the Elder.

Osiris — God of the dead and resurrection. First pharaoh of Egypt who was murdered by Set, resurrected by Isis, and became king of the afterlife. Every dead person hoped to become Osiris. Depicted as a mummified king with green or black skin.

Ptah — Creator god of Memphis. Created the world through thought and speech. God of craftsmen, architects, and builders. Depicted as a mummified man. Husband of Sekhmet.

Ra — The sun god. King of the gods, especially prominent during the Old Kingdom. Traveled across the sky daily in his solar boat and through the underworld each night. Frequently combined with other gods (Amun-Ra).

Sekhmet — Fierce lioness goddess. Daughter of Ra in many traditions. Goddess associated with war, plague, and healing. The Eye of Ra sent to punish rebellious humanity. Could cause or cure disease. Wife of Ptah.

Set — God associated with chaos, storms, deserts, violence, and foreigners. Brother and murderer of Osiris in the Osirian myth. Lost the kingship to Horus after their contest. Despite being antagonist in the Osiris myth, Set also served as protector who defended Ra's boat against Apep.

Shu — God of air and space. First god created by Atum. Held Nut (sky) and Geb (earth) apart. Father of Geb and Nut.

Sobek — Crocodile god. God of the Nile, fertility, protection, and military prowess. Could be dangerous or helpful depending on context.

Taweret — Hippopotamus goddess (with lion and crocodile features). Protected pregnant women and infants. Fierce appearance scared away evil spirits.

Tefnut — Goddess of moisture. First female goddess created by Atum. Twin/wife of Shu. Mother of Geb and Nut.

Thoth — Ibis-headed (or baboon) god of wisdom, writing, magic, and the moon. Scribe of the gods. Arbitrated the Horus–Set conflict. Inventor of hieroglyphs. Recorded the results of the heart-weighing ceremony.

Important Monsters and Beings

Ammit — "The Devourer." Composite creature with crocodile head, lion forequarters, and hippopotamus hindquarters. Waited by the scales of judgment to eat the hearts of those who failed, causing the "second death."

Apep (Apophis) — Giant serpent of chaos. Enemy of Ra who attacked the solar boat every night trying to prevent sunrise. Represented everything that opposed Ma'at. Could never be permanently killed.

Bennu Bird — Sacred bird (often depicted as a heron) associated with the sun, creation, and resurrection. The first living creature to appear on the primeval mound in some versions. Greek phoenix stories may derive from the Bennu.

Key Mythological Terms

Akh — The transfigured, glorified spirit that results when the ka and ba successfully reunite in the afterlife. The final, perfected form of the deceased who had passed judgment and achieved eternal life.

Ankh — Symbol of life. Carried by gods, often held to the pharaoh's nose to grant life.

Ba — The personality aspect of the soul. Depicted as a human-headed bird. Could travel between the tomb and the world but needed to return to the body.

Benben — The primeval mound that first emerged from the waters of Nun at creation. Atum stood on the Benben to begin creating the world. The pyramidion (capstone) atop pyramids and obelisks represented the Benben.

Canopic Jars — Four containers used during mummification to store the deceased's internal organs (liver, lungs, stomach, and intestines). Each jar was protected by one of the Four Sons of Horus.

Cartouche — An oval rope loop enclosing the pharaoh's names (prenomen and nomen). The oval symbolized the king's rule over everything the sun encircles.

Djed Pillar — Symbol of Osiris and stability. Represented his backbone.

Duat — The underworld. The dangerous realm of the dead that the sun traveled through each night. Full of gates, guardians, and challenges.

Ennead — The group of nine gods worshiped at Heliopolis: Atum, Shu, Tefnut, Geb, Nut, Osiris, Isis, Set, and Nephthys. The first several generations of creation who organized the cosmos.

Field of Reeds (Aaru) — The Egyptian paradise where the blessed dead lived eternally after passing judgment. An idealized version of Egypt with abundant harvests, perfect weather, and no death or suffering.

Heka — Magic, both as a concept and sometimes personified as a god. The power that allowed creation to happen and that gods, pharaohs, priests, and magicians could manipulate. Magic was integral to how the universe functioned in Egyptian belief.

Isfet — Chaos, disorder, and everything that opposed Ma'at. The force of destruction and entropy that constantly threatened cosmic order. Could only be held at bay through constant ritual and ethical behavior.

Ka — The life force or vital essence. Needed food and drink (the spiritual essence of offerings). Lived in the tomb and required the body to be preserved.

Ma'at — Cosmic order, truth, justice, balance, harmony. Both a goddess and the fundamental organizing principle of the universe. The opposite of Isfet (chaos).

Natron — A naturally occurring salt used to desiccate bodies during mummification. The deceased was packed in natron for forty days to remove all moisture.

Negative Confession — Declarations made by the deceased during judgment before Osiris and the forty-two judges. The deceased would recite sins they had not committed: "I have not killed, I have not stolen, I have not lied..."

Nu (Nun) — The primordial waters of chaos that existed before creation. Infinite, dark, and formless. The Benben mound emerged from Nu's waters, and creation began.

Ogdoad — The group of eight primordial gods worshiped at Hermopolis who represented the formless state before creation: Nun and Naunet (water), Heh and Hauhet (infinity), Kek and Kauket (darkness), and Amun and Amaunet (hiddenness).

Opening of the Mouth — A crucial ritual that brought statues and mummies "to life" by opening their mouths so they could breathe, eat, speak, and see. Priests used special tools to touch the mouth, eyes, ears, and nose, activating these senses magically.

Scarab — Beetle that represented transformation, rebirth, and the sun being pushed across the sky.

Sed Festival — Royal jubilee held after thirty years of rule to magically renew the pharaoh's power through ritual.

Serekh — A rectangular frame representing a palace façade, topped with the Horus falcon, that enclosed the pharaoh's Horus name (the first of his five royal names). One of the oldest royal symbols.

Shabti (Ushabti) — Small mummiform figurines buried with the dead to serve as magical workers in the afterlife. When the deceased was called to perform labor in the Field of Reeds, the shabti would answer instead. Wealthy Egyptians were buried with 401 shabtis.

Uraeus — The rearing cobra worn on the pharaoh's crown. Originally Atum's angry eye. Symbol of divine protection and royal authority.

Was Scepter — Staff with animal head and forked bottom. Symbol of power and dominion.

Wedjat Eye — The Eye of Horus. Symbol of wholeness, healing, and protection. Became one of Egypt's most common amulets.

Here's another book by Matt Clayton that you might like

Free Bonus from Captivating History (Available for a Limited time)

Hi History Lovers!

Now you have a chance to join our exclusive history list so you can get your first history ebook for free as well as discounts and a potential to get more history books for free!

Simply visit the link below to join.

Or, Scan the QR code!

captivatinghistory.com/ebook

Also, make sure to follow us on Facebook, X, and YouTube by searching for Captivating History.

References

Allen, James P. *Genesis in Egypt: The Philosophy of Ancient Egyptian Creation Accounts*. Yale Egyptological Seminar, 1988.

Allen, James P. *Middle Egyptian: An Introduction to the Language and Culture of Hieroglyphs*. Cambridge University Press, 2014.

Allen, James P. *The Ancient Egyptian Pyramid Texts*. Society of Biblical Literature, 2005.

Assmann, Jan. *The Search for God in Ancient Egypt*. Cornell University Press, 2001.

Bagnall, Roger S. *Egypt in Late Antiquity*. Princeton University Press, 1993.

Hart, George. *Egyptian Myths*. University of Texas Press, 1990.

Hart, George. *The Routledge Dictionary of Egyptian Gods and Goddesses*. Routledge, 2005.

Hornung, Erik. *Conceptions of God in Ancient Egypt: The One and the Many*. Cornell University Press, 1982.

Hornung, Erik. *The Ancient Egyptian Books of the Afterlife*. Cornell University Press, 1999.

Lesko, Barbara S. *The Great Goddesses of Egypt*. University of Oklahoma Press, 1999.

Mojsov, Bojana. *Osiris: Death and Afterlife of a God*. Blackwell Publishing, 2005.

Pinch, Geraldine. *Magic in Ancient Egypt*. University of Texas Press, 1994.

Pinch, Geraldine. *Egyptian Mythology: A Guide to the Gods, Goddesses, and Traditions of Ancient Egypt*. Oxford University Press, 2002.

Taylor, John H. *Death and the Afterlife in Ancient Egypt.* University of Chicago Press, 2001.

Teeter, Emily. *Religion and Ritual in Ancient Egypt.* Cambridge University Press, 2011.

Wilkinson, Richard H. *The Complete Gods and Goddesses of Ancient Egypt.* Thames & Hudson, 2003.

Image Sources

1   Jon Bodsworth, Copyrighted free use, via Wikimedia Commons,
    https://commons.wikimedia.org/wiki/File:Pyramidion-satellite-kh%C3%A9ops.jpg

2   https://commons.wikimedia.org/wiki/File:Geb,_Nut,_Shu.jpg

3   Sanjay ach, CC BY-SA 4.0 <https://creativecommons.org/licenses/by-sa/4.0>, via
    Wikimedia Commons, https://commons.wikimedia.org/wiki/File:Shabaka_
    Stone_at_the_British_Museum.jpg

4   SFEC_2009_POT-0008.JPG: S F-E-Cameronderivative work: JMCC1, CC BY-SA
    3.0 <https://creativecommons.org/licenses/by-sa/3.0>, via Wikimedia Commons,
    https://commons.wikimedia.org/wiki/File:Ogdoad_-_The_Place_of_Truth_-
    _Deir_el_Medina.jpg

5   Olaf Tausch, CC BY 3.0 <https://creativecommons.org/licenses/by/3.0>, via
    Wikimedia Commons, https://commons.wikimedia.org/wiki/File:Abydos_
    Tempelrelief_Sethos_I._36.JPG

6   A. Parrot, CC0, via Wikimedia Commons,
    https://commons.wikimedia.org/wiki/File:Horus_and_Seth_crowning_Ramesses_III,
    _detail_of_Horus.JPG

7   Jeff Dahl, CC BY-SA 4.0 <https://creativecommons.org/licenses/by-sa/4.0>, via
    Wikimedia Commons, https://commons.wikimedia.org/
    wiki/File:Eye_of_Horus_bw.svg

8   Jeff Dahl, CC BY-SA 4.0 <https://creativecommons.org/licenses/by-sa/4.0>, via
    Wikimedia Commons, https://commons.wikimedia.org/wiki/File:Re-Horakhty.svg

9   Jeff Dahl, CC BY-SA 4.0 <https://creativecommons.org/licenses/by-sa/4.0>, via
    Wikimedia Commons, https://commons.wikimedia.org/wiki/File:Thoth.svg

10 https://commons.wikimedia.org/wiki/File:Anubis_attending_the_
mummy_of_Sennedjem.jpg

11 Gunawan Kartapranata, CC BY-SA 3.0 <https://creativecommons.org/licenses/by-
sa/3.0>, via Wikimedia Commons,
https://commons.wikimedia.org/wiki/File:Bastet.svg

12 I, Rémih, CC BY-SA 3.0 <http://creativecommons.org/licenses/by-sa/3.0/>, via
Wikimedia Commons,
https://commons.wikimedia.org/wiki/File:Wall_relief_Kom_Ombo4.JPG

13 https://commons.wikimedia.org/wiki/File:Dendera_7_977.PNG

14 Museo Egizio in Turin (IT), CC0, via Wikimedia Commons,
https://commons.wikimedia.org/wiki/File:Amuleto_raffigurante_il_dio_Bes_1DSC49
45.tif

15 Metropolitan Museum of Art, CC0, via Wikimedia Commons,
https://commons.wikimedia.org/wiki/File:Statuette_of_the_Goddess_Taweret_MET_
DP243443.jpg

16 BVBurton, CC BY-SA 4.0 <https://creativecommons.org/licenses/by-sa/4.0>, via
Wikimedia Commons, https://commons.wikimedia.org/wiki/File:
Statue_of_Sobek_Ashmolean.jpg

17 Old Fund, CC0, via Wikimedia Commons,
https://commons.wikimedia.org/wiki/File:Statuette_of_the_god_Khnum,_steatite_-
_Museo_Egizio_Turin_C_513_p05.jpg

18 FDRMRZUSA, CC BY-SA 4.0 <https://creativecommons.org/licenses/by-sa/4.0>, via
Wikimedia Commons, https://commons.wikimedia.org/wiki/File:
Amun_post_Amarna_(azure_skin_color).svg

19 A. Parrot, CC0, via Wikimedia Commons,
https://commons.wikimedia.org/wiki/File:Mut_nursing_Seti_I.jpg

20 zolakoma, CC BY 2.0 <https://creativecommons.org/licenses/by/2.0>, via Wikimedia
Commons, https://commons.wikimedia.org/wiki/File:
Min_at_Karnak_Temple.jpg

21 https://commons.wikimedia.org/wiki/File:Egyptian_-_Ba_Bird_-_Walters_571472.jpg

22 https://commons.wikimedia.org/wiki/File:Ammit_BD.jpg

23 https://commons.wikimedia.org/wiki/File:27.1_Iaru.tif

24 https://commons.wikimedia.org/wiki/File:Nut1.JPG

25 Guillaume Blanchard, CC BY-SA 1.0 <https://creativecommons.org/licenses/by-
sa/1.0>, via Wikimedia Commons,
https://commons.wikimedia.org/wiki/File:Egypte_louvre_290.jpg

26 Osama Shukir Muhammed Amin FRCP(Glasg), CC BY-SA 4.0
<https://creativecommons.org/licenses/by-sa/4.0>, via Wikimedia Commons,
https://commons.wikimedia.org/wiki/File:Birth_and_Throne_cartouches_of_pharaoh
_Seti_I,_from_KV17_at_the_Valley_of_the_Kings,_Egypt._Neues_Museum.jpg